AGAINST THE ICE

AGAINST THE ICE

The Classic Arctic Survival Story

EJNAR MIKKELSEN

Foreword by
NIKOLAJ COSTER-WALDAU

Translated from the Danish by
MAURICE MICHAEL

STEERFORTH PRESS
LEBANON, NEW HAMPSHIRE

First published in Danish as *Farlig Tomandsfærd* in 1955 by Gyldendalske
Boghandel, Nordisk Forlag A/S, Copenhagen, Denmark

The publisher wishes to thank the Danish Polar Center for their assistance. All
photographs © Arctic Institut.

For information about permission to reproduce
selections from this book, write to:
Steerforth Press L.C., 31 Hanover Street,
Lebanon, NH 03766

Library of Congress Cataloging-in-Publication Data

Mikkelsen, Ejnar, 1880–
  [Farlig Tomandsfærd. English]
  Two against the ice / Ejnar Mikkelsen ; translated from the Danish by
Maurice Michael.— Steerforth Press ed.
     p. cm.
First published in Copenhagen : Gyldendal, 1955.
  ISBN 978-1-58642-334-6 (alk. paper)
  1. Mikkelsen, Ejnar, 1880—Journeys—Greenland. 2. Mikkelsen, Ejnar,
1880—Journeys—Arctic regions. 3. Greenland—Discovery and
exploration—Danish. 4. Arctic regions—Discovery and
exploration—Danish. 5. Alabama-expeditionen til Grønlands nordøstkyst
(1909-1912) 1. Title.
G743 .M63313 2003
919.8'204—dc21

                                    2002151150

FIRST EDITION

*To my loyal and cheerful companion in
North-east Greenland from 1909 to 1912*

IVER P. IVERSEN

CONTENTS

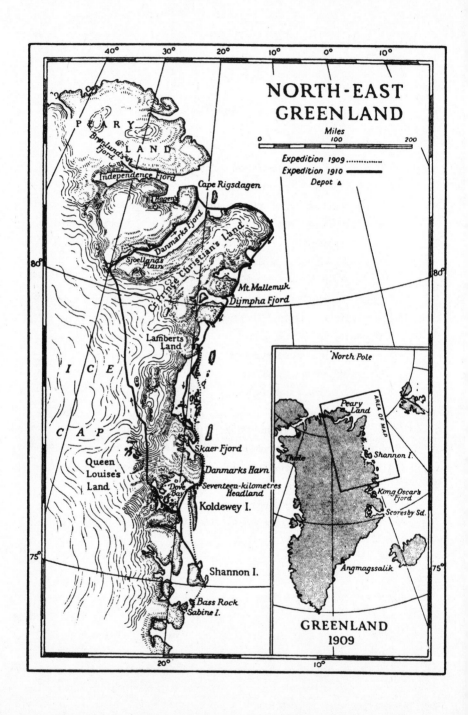

NORTH-EAST
GREENLAND

Miles
0   100   200

Expedition 1909 ....
Expedition 1910 ——————
Depot ▲

PEARY LAND

Brønlunds Fjord

Independence Fjord

Cape Rigsdagen

Hagen

Danmarks Fjord

Prince Christian's Land

Sjoellands Plain

Mt. Mallemuk

Dijmpha Fjord

Lamberts Land

ICE

CAP

Queen
Louise's
Land

Skaer Fjord

Danmarks Havn

Dove
Bay

Seventeen-kilometres
Headland

Koldewey I.

Shannon I.

Bass Rock
Sabine I.

GREENLAND
1909

North Pole

Peary
Land

AREA OF MAP

Thule

Shannon I.

Kong Oscar's
Fjord

Scoresby Sd.

Angmagssalik

FOREWORD

Queen Margrethe II of Denmark was working as the costume designer on an adaptation of a Hans Christian Andersen fairy tale that was being directed by a good friend of mine, Peter Flinth. During filming, she suggested that the memoir *Two Against the Ice* by Ejnar Mikkelsen would make a great movie. As a good, proud subject, Peter then sent a copy of the book to me.

It was 2011, and I was in Bolivia working on a fictional story about what would have happened if Butch Cassidy had lived out his days in the mountains there. Reading *Two Against the Ice*, I was struck by how reality often is stranger and more extreme than fiction. I have always been attracted to stories of explorers, tales of men and women who knowingly put themselves in harm's way in the pursuit of adventure and discovery. Mikkelsen's story grabbed hold of me and did not let go.

At the turn of the previous century, Arctic explorers — alpha males born with incredible self-belief in their abilities to achieve the impossible — traveled to places where nature held no respect for human life. Risking their lives to go where no man had gone before, many of them perished.

What set the story told in *Two Against the Ice* apart is that it featured two men who were the unlikeliest of companions. Ejnar Mikkelsen, an experienced explorer, ends up with a young mechanic, Iver Iversen, who only joined the expedition to Greenland that Mikkelsen was leading when its original mechanic turned out to be useless and a drunk. Iver had little if any ambition and zero experience in the Arctic.

So, when Mikkelsen needed a volunteer to accompany him on an arduous journey, it was surprising that it was the rookie Iversen who stepped up and threw himself into what he believed would be a few months of adventure.

These few months became three long years during which the two men battled the ice and deadly cold of the Arctic, managing to survive by virtue of companionship, friendship, and an unwavering trust in each other.

Within this book there is a particular moment that made me want to adapt it into a movie. It's a brief description of a postcard the two men find. The postcard depicts a group of young ladies in front of a building, and Ejnar and Iver choose imaginary girlfriends from among the members of the group. Ejnar picks only one and Iver picks three — after all, he was still young — and the ladies become very much real in their minds.

For me the anecdote of this simple postcard symbolized human perseverance. With nothing to look forward to but their inevitable demise, their minds created a fictional space to nurture. This provided blessed relief from the bleakness of their reality and amazingly, against impossible odds, they survived.

Ejnar and Iver suffered their one and only real falling-out when Iver shared a dream he had that included the girl Ejnar had chosen from the postcard to be his imagined beloved. Ejnar is consumed with anger and jealousy until finally they agree to give up their fictitious relationships and instead focus on their own very real companionship to see them through. The biggest threat they faced was breaking faith with each other while no more than a few feet apart, stranded in the far, far north in a tiny cabin on Shannon Island.

Ejnar Mikkelsen is a great storyteller who spins the tale of his journey with Iver Iversen into an account of what it means to be human. At the core of our existence, the most valuable experiences we ever have are with our companions in life.

We made the movie. My friend Peter directed, my writing partner and good friend Joe Derrick co-wrote the script. And a new friend, Baltasar Kormákur, co-produced. Friends and companions telling a story of friendship and companionship.

The film is an adaptation of Mikkelsen's remarkable book, and we have done all within our powers to do it justice. (The film is titled, simply, *Against the Ice*, and the publisher of the volume you are reading now chose to shorten the book's title in recognition of our effort.) My hope is that the film will serve as a good companion to the book.

If you watch the film on Netflix, I hope it will give you a sense of the preposterous beauty of Greenland, the unfathomable power of nature, and the fundamental human need for companionship. Enjoy.

Nikolaj Coster-Waldau
Copenhagen
October 2021

AGAINST THE ICE

CHAPTER I

The Start of a Greenland Expedition

An expedition is given up — Mylius-Erichsen perishes in the wilds —
Lord Northcliffe's offer and its consequences — Gay departure —
Ill-omens — We put in to Angmagssalik

The lot of the out-of-work explorer is not a happy one. His head teems with plans for new travels, but, poor man, he usually lacks the essentials for putting them into effect; for he is broke, stony broke, and often worse than that. I, at least, seem always to have been left with a number of larger or smaller bills to meet at the end of my expeditions, without having any idea where the money was to come from.

Of course there are fees to be earned for articles and lectures, and once in a while a cheque for a book about one's latest expedition, but they make little difference to a large deficit. Also, you feel that having returned to a civilized country after several years in the wilds, you are entitled to a period of ease and freedom from care.

Every civilized country has its kind people who feel sorry for the poor explorer with neither roots nor money, and hasten to tell him to be more sensible and to adopt a staid, quiet and profitable way of life instead of wasting his time running about the wilds. There was no need for those kind persons to tell me that; it had been all too obvious for a number of years. But what are you to do, when you have been born with eternal unrest in your body and are drawn to none but those parts of the world that sensible people regard as fit only for fools?

I made an honest attempt to be sensible and do as other young men did, but I was unable to suppress the restlessness within me. I became touchy and impatient, impossible to live with. I longed to be off again, away from the fretting ties of civilization, far in the north where one could live life to the full and be oneself. Such was my situation in the early summer of 1908 after returning home from a two-year expedition to the seas north of Alaska, where I had sought an undiscovered land, whose existence and position had not only been worked out in theory, but which had been seen by a couple of ships' crews and by Alaskan Eskimos. Or so they said.

Unfortunately the theorists were wrong in their calculations, and it is a mistake uncritically to accept everything people insist they have seen, for the land was not where it had been calculated to be. The discovery that it was not land, but an island of ice was reserved for the foolish youth of the future, those who joyfully hazard their lives in high-flying aeroplanes and use the stars as mile posts across the endless vault of the heavens, from which the view is so vast that those enormous floating ice-islands were at last discovered. Now they drift slowly with the current across the polar seas carrying scientists and technicians with them.

My outlook brightened one dark October day, when an old storm-whipped steamship chugged into Copenhagen and anchored in the roads. She was Mylius-Erichsen's expedition ship *Danmark* come home with great results from a two-years expedition to the then remote and unknown land of North-east Greenland. But the flag at the flagstaff aft was flying at halfmast, and the news soon spread that the great results obtained had cost three lives, including that of Mylius-Erichsen himself.

The experienced explorer knew, of course, that his life was not worth so very much once he had left civilization and been swallowed up in the wilds, for, unlike our young successors with their aeroplanes and wireless, we of the older generation had to manage entirely on our own, without the least possibility of obtaining outside help, if conditions proved worse than we had expected. We were aware of that, but it is nevertheless a blow when a flag at halfmast suddenly drags your thoughts from the struggles and events of everyday and compels them to fly far off to where friends and fellows have given their lives trying to wrest from the wilds some of their well-guarded secrets.

I knew two of the men for whom that flag flew: Mylius-Erichsen, a dauntless idealist, dreamer and poet, and the faithful Greenlander Jørgen

Brønlund; and my thoughts went back three or four years to the time when Mylius and I had had a lot to do with each other. He had been bent on Greenland, while my inclination was for Alaska, but we had talked a great deal about the expeditions we were planning, and for a time I was greatly tempted to let the unknown land north of Alaska remain unknown for a while longer and accept Mylius-Erichsen's offer to become commander of the expedition ship *Danmark*. We never managed to agree, though, for Mylius had some curious ideas (or so I thought them) about all members of the expedition being equal. Skipper and mess-boy should have the same say in all decisions: the expedition's motto was to be concord, and all that was done both on board ship and on land was to be agreed by everyone.

It all sounded so beautiful, yet, though I too was regarded as an incurable idealist, I was also a sailor, and as a seaman with some experience of ships and people, I could not believe in the right of consultation for all and the principle of equality either in a ship or on long and arduous sledging journeys. Mylius, however, would not give in, and I stuck to my point of view; thus nothing came of our proposed collaboration, and we went our separate ways in the North that was so endless in those days.

A month after *Danmark*'s return to Copenhagen, I was in London again trying my luck with the wealthy ones there. I was achieving very little, when one day I received a letter from Lord Northcliffe asking me to go and see him, as he wished to discuss with me a matter that ought to be of interest to me.

The wishes of the owner of the *Daily Mail* were royal commands to men like myself, who always hoped for a fair wind, and naturally I went, wondering what a mighty newspaper proprietor could have to discuss with me. He began to speak of the three men who had lost their lives in Greenland, of their diaries and journals, none of which had been found except for fragments of Jørgen Brønlund's, and of what these might contain; he spoke of English Polar explorers who had vanished and all that England had done to discover what had happened to them, and he ended by saying something to the effect that

I would never get money for another expedition to look for the land in the Beaufort Sea, but that he had a suggestion to make to me: I was to fit out an expedition to North-east Greenland and try to find the dead men's papers which must certainly contain interesting information. If I could find them he would publish them in the *Daily Mail*. He would pay the whole cost of the expedition. I had only to draw on him — and do my best.

That was an offer for you! Fancy being able to equip an expedition without first having to ring at innumerable doorbells to obtain the necessary money — which in the end always proved too little. However, as a Dane I did not like the idea of an Englishman paying for the expedition and of his money acquiring the rights to what three Danes had given their lives to achieve. It seemed scarcely right or reasonable, and I blushed for Denmark that Lord Northcliffe had offered to do what Denmark should have done — if the task was otherwise practicable.

After a sleepless night with all sorts of thoughts whirling in my head, I sent Lord Northcliffe a polite refusal, went back to Denmark and there announced cheerfully that I now knew what I wanted, that life had again acquired a purpose: that that summer I was going to Greenland to try and find Mylius-Erichsen's papers.

First I told my old friend and leader of my first expedition of what had transpired in London, and asked him to speak with the others on the Committee of the *Danmark* Expedition, of which he was a member, and see whether the Committee would give me its moral support where the public was concerned. It would certainly do me no harm to have some fine chaps to speak for me, for I was coming to be known as a pesterer.

I then had a meeting with the Committee, and having received its promise of both moral and active support, I then began to consider where the money was to come from. Once more I began the trudge from one to the other of those who both could and, I felt, should help to pay what it would cost for Denmark to do her duty to her three sons who had vanished in North-east Greenland. The Government had given a considerable grant to the *Danmark* Expedition, and I was now promised that it would cover half the cost of mine. After that it was relatively easy to obtain what I needed, which was 50,000 Crowns in all, and at the end of March 1909 the Committee was able to issue a statement announcing that the expedition was financially assured.

That was that, and I was glad that I had refused Lord Northcliffe's offer. At the same time, however, it ended my friendship with Lieutenant Koch, my companion on a former expedition, who had been second-in-command of the *Danmark* Expedition. Before leaving Greenland, Koch had sledged north to Lamberts Land, where he had found Jørgen Brønlund's body and in the dead man's pocket-book Hoeg-Hagen's sketch maps and Jørgen's diary which ended with the memorable and proud words:

> Succumbed at 79 fjord after attempting return across the inland ice in November. I arrived here in fading moonlight and could go no further because of frost-bitten feet and the dark. The others' bodies are to be found in the middle of the fjord in front of the glacier (about 12 miles). Hagen died 15 November Mylius about ten days later.

After that Koch thought that all further search for the dead men's bodies and any journals or notebooks they might have had, would be, and must remain, fruitless; also, that he, representing the remaining members of the *Danmark* Expedition, had done everything that could be done to elucidate the fate of their comrades.

The Committee of the *Danmark* Expedition, which had undertaken to act as my guarantor, shared my opinion that more ought to be done, and so presumably did the authorities, for otherwise Parliament would scarcely have agreed to pay half the cost of sending an expedition to search for further traces of the vanished men.

In Stavanger I found a suitable ship, *Alabama*. She was a Nordland yacht and roomy for a ship of her size, for she was only forty-five tons. She was cheap too, costing only 6000 Crowns, but the owner had stripped her of everything that was not nailed down.

I brought her to Copenhagen, where she was overhauled from keel to truck and a motor installed, relatively a monster of a thing, though only 18 h.p. Then, scrubbed and gleaming with new paint and finery, she was moored at the Royal Greenland Company's quay to take on equipment and provisions for sixteen months, but also so that we could show our fine ship to those who had made it possible to transform a Nordland yacht into as good an expedition ship, despite its size, as any that had sailed from Copenhagen with course set for the ice masses of East Greenland. People did not expect or require so much in those distant days.

Our friends seemed surprised that the name *Alabama*, strange to Danish eyes and ideas, still figured on the ship's quarter, now even carved on a mahogany name-board and the letters neatly gilded; but it is an old superstition of the sea that you should be very chary of changing a good ship's name before a long and dangerous voyage, for grief and misfortune may result from denying a ship her past. So she was allowed to retain her old name, though we all realized that we could very easily have found one far better suited to her mission than that she already bore.

The members of the Committee, grand-looking gentlemen wearing frock coats and glossy top hats as though going to a christening, came aboard to inspect the ship. The Prime Minister also wished to see what we had got with the government's grant, and the Director of the Greenland Administration came to assure us of the support Official Greenland would give us. The American Ambassador came, also in top hat, to admire the wonder and make sure for himself that it really was possible to fit out a Greenland expedition for the meagre sum we had said would be enough. As an American he could hardly believe it. Altogether we had so many visitors on board that the ship looked much smaller than she had before. Thus everyone else thought her far too little to endure so long a voyage.

When all outsiders had departed, the Chairman of the Committee asked me to assemble our small crew aft and he then read a message to us from King Frederick VIII. While he was reading it, a telegraph boy stood waiting on the quayside. His telegram was from Crown Prince Christian.

The good wishes and attention paid to us were almost overwhelming. When the commotion was all over and we were alone, I went to the little cabin where Lieutenant Vilhelm Laub, Lieutenant C. A. Jørgensen and I were to make ourselves comfortable on the voyage. Sitting there, my thoughts went back for a moment to my departure from Vancouver, when I set out on my last expedition in the little *Duchess of Bedford*, and how the Harbour Master's launch had pursued us carrying an anxious Chinaman loudly demanding payment for some trousers he had pressed and sponged, a whole two dollars, and how we had been unable to scrape that much together, even though we emptied all our pockets.

There could scarcely have been a greater contrast between then and now, and if good wishes counted for anything, then all should go well with us on our journey into distant North-east Greenland.

It was 1909 and summer was at its loveliest when the hour of departure struck and little *Alabama* headed out to sea on her long voyage to East Greenland, accompanied by good wishes and with hope and confidence at the wheel.

Three weeks later, and for a long time after that, it was as though all our efforts and hopes were to be frustrated by circumstances over which we had no control.

Our misfortunes began when we came to take over the fifty sledge dogs that had been bought for us in West Greenland and shipped to the Faroes in one of the Greenland Administration's boats. They had been good, strong animals, but the hardships of the voyage and perhaps thought-less and unwarrantable treatment had quite ruined them, so that, after consulting with the authorities, men who knew what they were talking about, we had to bring ourselves to shoot every one of them.

The second misfortune came with our Greenlander. He was to have come with us as hunter and to look after the dogs, but there he was in bed in one of our cabins with pneumonia, fighting for his life. The local doctor ordered him to be taken ashore at once, and so we lost him as well.

Without dogs we were not in a position to do anything, and I ought to have heeded Fate's warnings and renounced the attempt. But I have never liked the idea of turning back from a journey once begun, and after a week of conferring by telegraph with the Committee in Copenhagen we left the Faroes and steered for Angmagssalik, in the hope of a quick voyage and of obtaining the dogs we needed as a reward for the risk we were running, for such a trip was a dangerous undertaking so early in the year. However, all went well and we bought all the dogs the Eskimos could let us have. We now had as many as had been sent from West Greenland, but these dogs were nothing like as good, so small and puny that I felt very doubtful of them. Again I should have given up, but I took comfort from the thought that perhaps the dogs were better than they looked, poor comfort indeed.

That, however, was not the end of our misfortunes, far from it. The motor started giving trouble and then failed just when we needed it most. At first we told ourselves that these were the expedition's teething troubles, and we relieved our feelings in true sailor's fashion by cursing the motor to which we had been looking to take us through the pack ice. It was not long, however, before we began to wonder whether perhaps the motor itself was all right, and our real difficulty simply that our highly recommended mechanic was unable to keep it going. Our doubts gradually turned to certainty: our mechanic was definitely not up to his job and would have to be replaced by another and better, or else we must abandon the idea of reaching East Greenland so late in the year.

But where were we to get another and better man? For a third time I ought to have given up, for all these difficulties and delays had absorbed most of the short Greenland summer during which we should have achieved so much. Luckily the Danish Government's inspection ship *Islands Falk* was at Iceland, to which we came in a storm with our puny dogs, broken-down motor and useless mechanic. I bewailed my fate to the captain, and he, stout fellow, was only too ready to do what he could. The telegraph began to work; the Danish Admiralty was most considerate and after an exchange of telegrams the captain was able to say to his crew that any who wished was at liberty to volunteer as mechanic on board *Alabama*, and would earn the Admiralty's thanks for helping a good cause.

One man volunteered, I was told, just one. His name was Iver P. Iversen, and it seemed to be agreed that if anyone could get a machine to work as it was meant to, that man was Iversen. This sounded better, and I went aboard *Islands Falk* and asked to see him. He came down to the captain's cabin, short and slight and not much to look at, but he was all afire to get at the motor which a brother mechanic had given up and which now lay in innumerable pieces in our little engine-room.

"Well, what do you say, Iversen?" the captain asked. "Can you master the motor? And will you go with the expedition up there?"

Iversen replied unhesitatingly that he would, and that if there were no parts missing, he would get that motor going all right. And even if there was a piece or two missing, he would patch it up quite satisfactorily. And he would like to go with the expedition as well. He had wanted to do that for a long time, ever since he had read the articles on Ejnar Mikkelsen's expedition that came out in *Familie Journal*.

So it was decided. Iversen could not possibly be less talented and energetic than the mechanic we had had so far.

Some hours later, while it was still night, *Islands Falk* passed us the end of a hawser to tow us northwards, and Iversen came across to little *Alabama* after a protracted leave-taking from his gay shipmates in the trim man-of-war.

Once we were clear of land, Iversen gave us a cheery nod and climbed down to the motor. Shortly afterwards we heard the clang of swift hammer strokes on ringing steel, the rasp of files, the clatter of engine parts being shoved here and there, all of which was accompanied either by merry song or thoughtful whistlings, and interrupted by short periods of silence, as Iversen pondered his problems. Life had suddenly come to an engine-room that till then had been so dead.

Laub came to me as I stood enchanted, listening to the sounds of bubbling energy and activity coming up from the black hole, and we agreed that Iversen certainly knew how to work. Not till after a day and a night's towing, when the time had come to part company with *Islands Falk*, did Iversen stick his head out of the engine room. He was black and badly in need of sleep; he was bruised from the impact of slithering, heavy bits of iron, but he showed his white teeth in a joyous grin and said: "Well, skipper, just give the word and the motor will start."

To our great joy and surprise the motor really did start, and what is more, it went without hissing, coughing or clattering, or emitting suffocating fumes. And, wonder of wonders, it only stopped when it should, and obediently started again when we had need of its power.

Now at last things seemed to be improving, but already all these unforeseen difficulties and setbacks had cost us a month and a half of the best of the summer weather, of which we should have made the utmost use. By the time *Islands Falk* left us a little north of Iceland, we should have long since been through the ice, which we could not expect even to meet for another two or three days.

CHAPTER II

East Greenland at Last

A hard struggle with pack ice — Winter harbour —
Men and animals prepare for winter — A change of plan

It was already late in the year when above the western horizon we saw the yellow-white sheen in the sky that betrays the proximity of ice. The weather was the worst imaginable for trying to negotiate pack ice. Low torn clouds poured across the heavens like a beaten enemy, pursued by a howling north storm that sent scurry after scurry of snow to envelop us and the wind-whipped seas that broke in foaming surf against the edge of the ice.

Undoubtedly, the only defensible course of action would have been to stand off and wait for better weather before entering the ice. But beyond the fringe of crushed ice and noisy breakers we could glimpse long lanes of open water between the drifting floes, a negotiable path towards the west and the coast of Greenland.

It was a hypnotising, tempting sight, too tempting for an impatient person; so, when I saw the hint of an opening in the fringe of violently pitching floes, my eagerness to get to the west sent caution and care to the winds: the opportunity must not be wasted. While I climbed aloft in order to try from the masthead to guide the ship through the narrow leads between the floes, Iversen started the motor; then with sheets let fly and the motor at full speed we roared towards the edge of the ice, where the breakers were making as much noise as they will on the west coast of Jutland in an on-shore storm.

Too late I began to regret my rashness; too late I realized that there was almost no hope that we should come with whole skins through that confusion of ice and thundering breakers fifty yards to leeward. But we could not now get back to the open sea, for both sea and wind were dead against us. There was nothing to do but hope that Fate would smile on us, and that we might slip through a short narrow channel between two large floes, while they were still lying apart in that seething commotion. Once through that channel we were bound to find things easier, for a couple of hundred yards in from the edge the ice looked navigable.

Our luck deserted us, however, just at the crucial moment, and on the crest of a wave *Alabama* ran at a speed of six or seven knots on to a spur of ice, struck so hard that hull and mast groaned, and there she was stuck fast on the ice amidst seething breakers.

The sails flapped violently as we swung up into the wind that clamoured round us. The surf broke in over the rail and washed to and fro across the deck. The dogs squealed with fright at the water, the reports of the cracking sails, and the thunderous blows that shook the ship and made every plank in her hull groan.

It seemed the end.

Luckily, we had no time to think about that. I had to get down from the violently swaying mast as fast as I could and help the others on deck to ward off the worst bumps, and, if possible, get the ship afloat again. We toiled with long boat hooks, ran about on heaving floes that seas were continually sweeping, trying to get ropes made fast to protruding pieces of ice, so as to coax the ship into the open and more or less calm water farther in among the ice floes.

We had better luck than I deserved, and after an hour's struggling, with the loss of the ship an all too obvious possibility, we got her through the narrow barrier of ice and into relatively clear water.

Naturally, the ship had suffered minor damage from this rough treatment, a split rudder-stock, for example. But did that really matter? Whatever the damage, as long as the ship would float and could be steered, she would still serve her purpose, which was to bring us to some place on the coast from which we could start out on our sledge journeys. Afterwards we would always be able to get back home to Denmark one way or another, whether we had a ship of our own or not.

There then followed happy days when we made good progress

among the ice-floes which were many miles in extent, and days of
storm with pack ice that clasped our little ship with so hard a grip, that
it was touch and go whether she would be crushed like an eggshell or
come free and get into the open water we could see so close ahead. And
so, one day late in the summer, we reached the coast of East Greenland.

We were a good bit farther south than we had reckoned, some two
hundred miles in fact, and for that we would have to suffer when we
began sledging. There was nothing to be done about it, however, for
the ice was packed tight as far north as we could see, and the few small
gaps in the pack that could be glimpsed here and there kept altering
with change of tide and current and led nowhere, except possibly into
new dangers similar to those from which we had just escaped. Thus,
we made a virtue of necessity and were as cautious as it was possible to
be. The days were growing shorter and the autumnal storms beginning
seriously to harass everything that moved on land or ice, so we crept
circumspectly in between ice and skerries and found a haven, which
was as far north as we could get with our ship. There we let go the
anchor, stretched hawsers to the land and prepared the ship for the
winter by stretching her main sail across her from stem to stern like a
tent.

The migrant birds had long since flown to the fair lands of the south;
and there were not even the harsh cries of the sea birds to be heard, for
an ice-covered sea gave them no food. Now and again we could hear
the hoarse croak of a solitary, hungry raven, gliding like the white owls
through the clear quivering air high above our heads, scanning the land
with its sharp eyes in search of lemmings, a frightened hen ptarmigan
(though preferably ptarmigan chicks), or a leveret, all of which was
welcome fare in the harsh days of autumn.

Lone polar bears caught the heavenly smells from our little camp
from afar and paid us visits by both day and night, hoping to be able to
share in whatever it was that smelled so good. The dogs gave tongue
and bravely tackled the great animals that snarled and struck at their
puny adversaries with paws that on one occasion sent one of them
flying with blood pouring from great wounds. At that the other dogs

fell upon the battered bleeding wretch and zealously finished off what the bear had so well begun.

We, of course, could not refrain from taking a hand in the gory fight. Rifles cracked, bullets whined, and as a rule the bear discovered too late that we demanded the death penalty for its attempt to purloin what was undeniably ours. And when the bear eventually collapsed in a pool of blood, we had to wield our whips to keep the dogs off it. Fresh steaming bear's blood can so excite a half-starved sledge dog that it will forget all fear of its master, and if it has once snatched a lump of fresh bear's meat, it will defend it to the last shred, and almost choke itself in an attempt to swallow it whole, before the others can wrest the prize away.

On shore we now and again saw a large whitish animal sneaking about in our vicinity. It resembled a large dog, and was in fact one of the greedy polar wolves which have since disappeared from East Greenland, though in those days they were quite numerous. Our dogs almost always sensed their presence and attacked in a solid bunch with howls and snarls and much barking. Then there was war between brothers, but as a rule it was all over by the time we reached the battlefield with our rifles, and the torn, bleeding dogs, whimpering and cowed, sought protection beside us. We never managed to hit a wolf, for they sneaked off as soon as they saw help coming.

There were foxes, too, both white and blue. They gobbled up the remains of any food the dogs might miraculously have over-looked, and when a bear had been laid low, they came and gorged on its meat and blood side by side with the dogs.

There was plenty for us to attend to as the darkness, cold and howling storms of autumn began in earnest. The dogs had to be tended, sledges lashed, provisions weighed and packed for our impending sledge journey to Lamberts Land, and there was also a certain amount to be done on the ship. We took it in turns to be cook, and at night we slept the sleep of tired young men, disturbed only by the weird sounds as the frost bit deep into the hull and imprisoned moisture froze and burst frost cracks in the planks, or when the ice was fissured by the frost and screamed like a man in distress as it split.

The harder it froze, the more we rejoiced, for we had a long sledge journey ahead of us and the earlier we could make a start the better. The many difficulties of my winter's journey along the coast of Alaska were still so fresh in my memory that I wanted to get this journey over before it became too cold and dark. In addition, we had to cross the open sea to Koldewey Island, no great distance when measured with protractors on the chart — only forty miles — but uncomfortable in prospect, when we sat on a hilltop near our winter harbour and stared out across the sea towards the north; for the sea was in continual rapid movement, and where there appeared to be a practical path for sledges one day there was almost open water the next. How were we to get across that stretch of ice and water with sledges and dogs?

Was it even possible to get as far as Lamberts Land with sledges so late in the year? Soon there would be snowstorms blowing day after day; the going would always be heavy, and the darkness so intense that we would be able to sledge for only a few hours each day. It was 330 miles to Lamberts Land, and we hoped to be able to return. Even under ideal circumstances seven hundred miles is a long way to sledge. And we would have everything against us. Could it even be done, conditions being what they were?

The attempt ought to be made all the same, as we were now forced to alter our original plans completely, because the delays we had suffered at the Faroes and Iceland, and then the voyage to Angmagssalik for new dogs, had cost us more than a month of the best period for navigating the ice. As a result, we had reached the coast of East Greenland so late that we had to consider ourselves lucky to have got as far north as we had, and to have found a relatively snug winter-harbour at the north-eastern point of Shannon Island, though that unfortunately was still some 130 miles south of Danmarks Havn at which we had been aiming.

The way things had turned out, I felt, compelled us to attempt the sledge journey to Lamberts Land, and my rash readiness to take a chance drowned the voice of common sense, telling me that the hard frost might easily come early and make the sea ice relatively safe to sledge on, that the autumnal storms could be few and of short duration, and that, since the moon would be full at the time we could expect to reach Lamberts Land, not even the darkness should put insuperable difficulties in the way of our search.

I explained to my companions the considerable difficulties we must expect to meet on our journey. Jørgensen was perfectly prepared to accompany me, difficulties or no difficulties, and then one day Iversen came up to me and said: "Look here, the motor isn't going to be used for the time being, so I'm out of a job. May I come on the sledge journey to Lamberts Land?"

Iversen was the smallest and slightest of my companions, but there was no doubt whatever of his determination, strength and thirst for adventure. It was true that he did not now have anything particular to do on board; he had volunteered of his own accord and laughed at all the warnings which my common sense still kept giving me and which I now passed on to him. "Just you go where you want to go," he said. "I'll keep up with you all right, in spite of open water, storm, snow, darkness or any other devilry!"

So it was decided. After that, all that remained was to see that everything was ready for the journey and then to wait for an early severe frost, which we hoped would bridge the sea between Shannon and Koldewey Islands and lay a solid covering of ice all along the open coast northwards from Danmarks Havn.

We *had* to get to Lamberts Land then, autumn or no autumn. So why think so much of all the things that spoke against making the attempt? It had to be made and that was all there was to it.

CHAPTER III

Sledging in Darkness and Storm

Hard sledging conditions — The dogs die of exhaustion — Darkness,
storm and driving snow — Lamberts Land — Jørgen Brønlund's grave —
Hurricane at Danmarks Havn — Frost bite — We arrive back

From the beginning of September the sledges stood loaded and ready
to leave, and we began trying to accustom the dogs to go more or less
peacefully together in teams that we made up from those we thought
best fitted for the long journey, irrespective of which companions the
dogs themselves preferred. It cost us a deal of sweat and shouting,
for dogs are refractory brutes; and our whips had to fall heavily on
the obstinate ones which tried to get out of doing the work for which
they were bred, and which yelped with pain as the lash struck them or
howled with longing to join the gay gang of their unharnessed fellows.

It was the equinox before we at last got away, but in spite of everything
that journey went much better than our pigheadedness deserved. Every
day we sledged over thin, yielding ice that all too often broke under the
sledges or was burst by an inquisitive playful narwhal, frolicking in the
cold water and breaking the shining crust of the ice with its back or long
unicorn's tooth; fascinating to see, but highly dangerous. Often the ice was
so thin that we could see swimming narwhals through it, and that was not
so pleasant. Time and again we had to spend slow hours in cold and driving snow waiting for the current to bring the new ice together and thus
build a horribly frail bridge between the drifting ice-floes, across which
we could go in relative safety with our sledges and belongings.

When the weather compelled us to halt, or if the darkness put
further sledging out of the question, we almost always managed to find
a relatively solid floe on which to pitch tent, and that was a joy indeed
to people who had so few joys as we did on that journey.

The dogs had a hard time of it, for it was exhausting work hauling the heavy sledges over the salty surface of the new ice on which the runners stuck. Splinters of the new ice, as sharp as glass, cut the dogs' pads to pieces, so that the snow in their tracks was tinged with blood; and the occasional duckings they had in the icy water were enough to rob even the most intrepid dog of its courage. Altogether it was a nightmare journey for our poor whimpering dogs, and the torment of it drained their strength and broke their courage long before we sledged into Danmarks Havn.

By that time one dog had already died, most probably of over-work, and several were so weak they looked as if they would go the same way. Thus, whether we liked it or not, after that journey of sixteen days, which ought not to have taken more than five, we had to give the dogs some days' rest at the *Danmark* Expedition's hut, which lay on some flat grassland between the ice of the sea and the mountains inland.

My companions and I had had nearly as hard a time as the dogs, and we also needed a rest, but tempting though that was, we could not help casting glum looks at the swiftly lengthening darkness, which was becoming more and more threatening as the days passed, stormy and with driving snow and relative warmth; and all that at a time of year when we had every right to expect severe frost and sparkling stars. The moon could not fail us, as everything else had so far, and it did occasionally show us its encouraging face between the scudding clouds, promising more light as soon as it had attained full stature and climbed higher into the heavens — at the same time as the days grew darker.

We dared not stay long in Danmarks Havn, and after four days of rest and security, we again headed north. All the time we battled against storm and dirty weather, sledging across either brittle new ice or violently packed old ice filled with pitfalls full of soft snow, so deep that we often sank up to our waists, while at times there was little more than the dogs' heads and tails to be seen above the surface.

It was arduous sledging. Darkness fell earlier every day as we struggled northwards towards even deeper darkness; and the driving snow prevented us making out where we were. The dogs grew rapidly weaker and weaker. They had a worse time of it in that hard autumn weather than any dogs I had ever seen. And what was worst of all, the glowing disc of the sun, which seemed to have no heat but cold in it, was sinking with horrifying speed towards the southern horizon, dropping a sun's diameter or two each time we saw it. On October 25, a calm, clear day, we saw the sun for the last time in 1909.

The sun made a lovely sight glowing in the midst of a vast expanse of orange red that imperceptibly turned into a delicate green shimmer, which, in its turn, merged with the blue of the sky high above the horizon where the stars were already beginning to sparkle. But the northern arch of the heavens was dark, black right down to the horizon, grim and menacing. And it was into that black vault that our way led. It would soon be all round us.

We halted a moment in our laborious march, so that we could say goodbye to the sun, which we were not to see again till towards the end of February. So it sank below the horizon, sending its last shafts of fire across ice and land, kindling a brief blaze among the massive mountains deep within the inland ice and lending a fleeting warm colour to the black mountains round us; and we bowed our heads as though a dear friend had died and his coffin just been lowered into the ground. We felt horribly alone and abandoned in the encompassing desolation. Our shadows ran from us towards the north, indicated the way we had to go — and vanished. The colours round us faded. The mountains stood black, both near us and in the distance, and even the ice now looked different from when the sun was shining on it and casting shadows, which have more effect on a man's state of mind than is generally realized.

The dogs whimpered under the lash of the cold, and when we went to move on again one of them was dead, dead of exhaustion. Another got to its feet with difficulty, pulled for an hour or so, stumbled, fell, lay a moment looking at us with handsome imploring eyes; then it rose laboriously but pulled no more: walking with loose trace, it fell for the last time and died an hour later.

We quartered the two dead dogs so that the others might live, for their flesh could not help being a bit more nourishing than the excrement and sealskin straps the dogs ate whenever there was a chance; and so our caravan toiled on again towards the north and the darkness. High above our heads a full moon swam past the throng of the stars, lighting our way even though its bright beams froze us to the quick.

There followed arduous days with endless toil and dying dogs, when we started long before the faint daylight began and camped in the evening by the gleam of a little lantern. But Lamberts Land was near. Its grim, vertical mountains towered just ahead of us and always we had with us the thought of the three men, who almost three years before to the day had struggled through the dark to the gates of death with frost eating at their hands and feet.

I remembered how gay and confident Mylius had been in sunny Copenhagen before he went to Greenland and I to Alaska, and I thought of his last apathetic effort before he collapsed from exhaustion with the same evil landscape before him as we now had close at hand. And I thought of Jørgen Brønlund and how he had come to me three or four years before and said: "I have promised to go with Mylius wherever he goes, and I will not break my word to him. I am going with him, but I wish you all possible success on your journey."

This faithful Greenlander had kept his word to the bitter end. Then, in the waning moonlight, he had left his companion's body somewhere in front of the glacier we could just glimpse in the gathering darkness, and continued on alone. Each of his tottering steps from his companion's camping place to the land ahead of us, which he reached with frost gnawing at his feet, must have cost him tremendous effort and torment. But he was determined to reach a place where his body and the information he carried about the unknown land, information that the three had given their lives to obtain, might stand a chance of being found, as they were some months later by Lieutenant Koch.

Wishing to be alone with my memories of dead friends, I sledged slightly ahead of the others for the last of the way; I reached the coast and sledged on slowly level with the land, my head full of all sorts of melancholy thoughts. Then I caught sight of foxes' tracks, first one, then many of them radiating like spokes from a small hole in the snow and extending far out across ice and land. The tracks showed that several foxes had been coming and going to and from a lair lying beneath the black hole in the snow. That hole struck me as a thing of horror, the horror of death, or, as conditions had been three years before, it was rather the entrance to the world of peace and rest.

I was convinced that beneath the white covering with its little black hole from which the foxes' tracks radiated across the desolate dead, white land, lay the mortal remains of Jørgen Brønlund; that it was there where I was standing that the faithful Greenlander had reached his journey's end, sunk down exhausted, overcome by the cold and the solitude. Even so, by the fading light of the moon, he had managed with numbed hands to write that moving account of the sledge party's misfortune, and so lain down to sleep the last sleep after so placing his diary that neither wild animals nor the raging gusts of winter could wrest it from his body once that had stiffened in death.

The others caught me up and, as their dogs dropped exhausted, I pointed to the hole and said, "We have reached our goal in this trackless land. There lies Jørgen Brønlund."

It was clear and still as we put up our tent. The effort had been great and we found little to say. The full moon shone, the stars twinkled and the northern lights flickered across the sky. Around us all was silent and quiet, the stillness of death and utter exhaustion, except for the heavy breathing of the dogs, which were too tired and weary of life to raise their heads, even when a fox darted out of the hole, halted a moment in horror at all that it saw and then vanished in great bounds.

The next day — as there was no day there in Lamberts Land, where day and night were almost equally dark, it is perhaps better to say: when the necessary number of hours had passed — we dug the snow away from Jørgen Brønlund's body and found a bag with a calendar and a pocket-book in which there were a couple of sketches of Mylius-Erichsen and Høeg-Hagen, some views of Danmark Fjord and a few leaves with writing in Eskimo, some utensils and cartridges, and finally, near the body, some tins of pemmican and other food.

We gathered stones, as many big ones as we could manage, and piled them over the body which we had wrapped in a shroud that Fru Mylius-Erichsen had given us, asking us to use it to cover the body of her husband or of his friend, Jørgen Brønlund. Thus we made a little grave-chamber, which the foxes could not break into and which would long stand as a monument, however poor, to a fine and gallant Greenlander. He had given his life in order to remain true to his word and to the Danish companions with whom he had journeyed into the unknown. Together they had dispersed the darkness which since the day of creation had lain over that part of North-east Greenland, which he had helped Mylius-Erichsen and Høeg-Hagen to travel and map. Those three brave men had suffered greatly, and in the end they had paid the most bitter price that man can pay for the privilege of seeing unknown land around him — and making it known.

It was a suitable resting-place for that much travelled Greenlander. Behind him towered the dark, almost vertical mountains, and in front of him lay the ice-clad sea. From his last resting place you could see the way that he and his companions must have come down from the hostile inland ice, and the place where Mylius-Erichsen and Høeg-Hagen had sunk exhausted and died "in the middle of the fjord, in front of the glacier, about ten miles."

If we were to find the other two bodies and their diaries, we would have to follow the land until we reached the glacier, out from which the two were supposed to lie; then we must continue till we were ten miles out from the glacier, at the spot whence Jørgen Brønlund had so painfully stumbled on frost-bitten feet. Luckily the weather was still and clear; the full moon was shining and lit up the landscape, and we were able to see quite far by its bright, unreal light. Leaving the sledges, we continued on foot, which we did so as to keep as close a contact as possible with the coast and the ice, and also because our dogs were dead tired and had to rest.

To our surprise we found extensive floes of new ice wherever we went "in the middle of the fjord in front of the glacier," and it soon became obvious that during the previous summer the old sea ice must have been broken up as far in as the glacier itself. It was therefore hopeless to search the ice, for if the three men's last camp had been on the sea-ice, as Jørgen Brønlund had written in his diary describing their last days, their bodies must either have drifted away with the old sea ice when the storms and waves of autumn broke it up, or have sunk into the sea when the ice melted in the summer sunshine.

There was no trace of the men's gear or of a camp on land either, and after spending three days in the area, luckily with good weather and bright moonlight, it was perfectly clear that any further search would be pointless.

Nor could we wait longer, for bad weather was threatening and we had to get away. The clouds were hanging low, so we struck camp and set off southwards, away from the horrible darkness that blotted out all the unevennesses in the very rough ice and compelled us to stumble along blindly, unable even to see where we were treading. The moon was now less than half and shed little light: we could see that sledging south was going to be even more difficult than the journey north, and that had been bad enough.

The only comfort we had to cling to was the hope that the everlasting storms would now blow our way, instead of being against us as on the journey north. That would have been a great help. But whether the journey were to prove easier or harder, we had to make a start, for there was no time to lose if we were to hope ever to get back to the ship.

It was a long way we had to go, and the dogs were almost dead beat. Two of them died while we were at Lamberts Land, and when we set off back southwards several others were unable to tighten their traces; they staggered as they walked and stumbled repeatedly. They could not go on. One of them lay motionless on the sledge and would soon be dead. Three dogs died on the first day of our homeward journey, and the next morning while we were cooking our Spartan breakfast in the tent and Iversen was busied outside preparing for departure, I heard him exclaim: "Now devil take me, have you ever seen the like of that? Max, God help me, has eaten Devil!"

I knew well enough that the dogs were dreadfully hungry, but that they were so hungry that they would attack a weaker fellow and eat its thin body was a thing I had never experienced before, nor thought possible. It was ghastly and boded us no good.

Devil was dead, and that was not such a loss, for he was a bad dog who stole from his companions and shirked his work, if he could see his way to do so; but what was much worse was that Max, a big, strong and willing dog, one of our best, over-ate himself on Devil and died of it before the day was out.

To add to the day's difficulties we had a violent snowstorm. The snow swirled across the ice covering it with a thick, soft layer, through which we and the dogs had to wade, laboriously dragging the sledges behind us. Even worse was in store, for when we camped we discovered that our last tin of paraffin had leaked and a considerable quantity of the precious stuff run out on to the snow. This meant that until we reached our most northerly depot and could get more paraffin, we must have hot food and drink only once a day. That was almost the worst of all.

It was a ghastly journey. We pressed on as hard as we could, fully conscious of the fact that we were fighting for our lives; and when you are doing that, you can accomplish wonders. Our provisions were almost at an end and our strength was not what it had been. When at length we reached Danmarks Havn with its hut, warmth and food, we even expressed a hope that a storm might compel us to stay there for a day or two, both for the dogs' sakes and our own. Scarcely had the words crossed our lips than a storm was howling and racing across land and ice in violent gusts, flinging pebbles and crust-ice against the hut, while we sat snugly indoors with the dogs, resting, eating and sleeping, enjoying the savage fury of the storm which increased till it reached hurricane force. It was not until the ninth day after reaching Danmarks Havn that we were able to continue our journey.

By this time we were really anxious. The darkness was lengthening at a disturbing pace, and it was going to be very difficult groping our way across the pitfalls of the ice — if indeed there was any ice, for it seemed more than probable that the violent storm had broken it all up and swept it far out to sea. If the ice were not broken, however, we ought to be able to make a fairly quick journey back to Shannon, for the long rest had allowed the dogs to recover. They were comparatively brisk and frisky as we harnessed them to the sledges and hopefully set off towards the faint gleam of light that, like a beacon in the darkness, showed us the direction in which we should go. In the centre of that gleam lay our ship, some 130 miles away in the south.

Our hopes of a quick end to that journey, on which everything had gone against us right from the very first, were disappointed as soon as we got outside the Danmarks Havn and came to the storm-tossed sea ice, where soft white snow was lying several feet deep between the great packs of ice that we had to cross, and we sank deep into it. Although the dogs were well rested, they could not haul the sledges through the soft snow, scarcely even with a man to help, and things went black before our eyes as the three of us hauled on the sledges to move them no more than a few yards. This was such a labour and we were so fagged that, despite the cold and our anxiety to press on, we had to stop for a breather nearly every ten minutes.

So we toiled southwards yard by yard, and the twilight had turned into the deep darkness of night long before exhaustion forced us to stop and pitch our tent only very few miles from Danmarks Havn. The shortness of the distance we had covered was bad enough, but that was not the extent of the day's worries. Once the dogs had been fed and we had gobbled up our pemmican and got ready for bed by pulling off our moccasins and stockings, it was discovered that both of Jørgensen's feet were badly frost-bitten. All the toes and the beginning of the foot were swollen and of the yellow, waxen colour of a corpse; rime crystals glittered on the skin.

Horrified, we asked how he could have got so badly frost-bitten. He thought that it must have been shortly after we set out that morning, when he had trodden through into a fissure filled with water, and the water had run into his moccasins. He had not paid particular attention to it, especially as the first searing pain in his feet quickly passed off; and even though his feet had seemed to become strangely insensible afterwards, he had said nothing so as not to waste precious time.

We spent most of the night rubbing his feet and warming them, and by degrees we did get a little life back into some of the toes. But when we had done all that could be done and crept into our sleeping bags, I felt pretty certain that Jørgensen would not be able to come on the big sledge journey across the inland ice that we planned for the spring.

I was quite certain of this when we removed the bandages a week later and saw the blue-coloured toes that were the all too evident signs of frost-bite. Iversen thought the same as I did, for a while later, as I sat on a hummock of ice during one of our all too frequent rests, he came up to me in the gloom and asked if I thought Jørgensen's feet would be all right by the spring. Unfortunately, I replied, I did not. Iversen paused, thumped his leg with his whip once or twice, then said: "That's what I thought. But if you like, I'll gladly go with you across the inland ice to Danmarks Fjord. It can't be much worse a journey than the one we can almost see the end of now."

A stout fellow, Iversen!

We toiled and struggled southwards, sledging in storms, snow and darkness so black that I had to let my leader dog go ahead on a long trace and leave her to find the best way through the jumble of ice. By doing that I could be sure of warning in time and not drive into deep holes or vainly try to force the sledge up packs that were yards high, yet impossible to see in that darkness without shadows. We waded through deep, soft snow which would bear neither us, the dogs, nor the sledges which sank deep into the yielding stuff and were continually capsizing, when it took the combined efforts of Iversen and myself to right them. We sledged over old ice with hummocks yards high and holes yards deep. We hauled the sledges across new ice that was solid enough, but covered with slush saturated with salt, and this penetrated the soles of our moccasins, through our thick wool socks, right to our icy feet that winced at the cold. It was good that they did, for then we knew that our toes had not yet become frost-bitten. That salt ice was a hell both for us and for the few dogs we still had left; but there was no escaping it, for in the darkness we could not see whether we should go to the right or to the left to avoid its sting. We just had to keep a more or less straight course towards our goal beneath the twinkling stars in the south, and take what the ice had to offer us with what equanimity we could muster — which was not much.

Our dogs were utterly exhausted. Although we had stayed too long in Danmarks Havn, the rest had not been long enough to restore the dogs' strength, and one after the other dropped in its traces, killed by the wet and by the effort of helping us to haul the sledges those last seventy miles or so of the seven hundred we had sledged. Dead, they were skinned and cut up and given to the others which still had spirit enough to wish to eat. It was not much exaggeration when, one day after a rest, Iversen called out to me as I moved off: "Hi! Wait a bit! Don't go off into the dark till I've got my dogs propped on their feet and can induce them to move."

My leader dog, the incomparable Girly, and I were in the lead, trying to find the easiest way through the darkness. Behind me I could make out the second sledge, driven by Iversen, who flung his weight into the trace over his shoulder whenever the sledge had to negotiate the slightest unevenness, toiled and fought to keep up with the lighter, leading sledge. In the rear came Jørgensen who had to cling to the uprights in order not to fall, for his feet would scarcely carry him and were so painful that every step was like being cut with knives.

We were a pitiable little procession. The dogs no longer whined, did not even snarl at each other; only now and again did plaintive gasps come from the poor brutes when the going became too heavy or the salt slush too biting. My two companions had still not lost their sense of humour, for now and again Iversen would strike up, and Jørgensen bravely join in and intone some lines of an old psalm used at weddings: "How lovely it is together, together . . ."

Naturally it was. At any rate it was better than being quite alone in that hell of darkness, ice, snow, storm and cold; but, as things were, it took a good deal of courage and confidence to be able to sing at all. I felt no desire to do so.

At length we caught a glimpse of the mountains on Shannon during the twilight of noon, and that spurred us to renewed efforts. For the next two or three days the land seemed to get no nearer, but then all at once the black mass of mountain had heaved itself up over the horizon and blotted out the lowest of the stars. It could not be long now; one more night in our sleeping bags that were frozen when we got in and later running with moisture, and then? . . . The toil, the effort and the struggle to get through had been so great that we could scarcely believe that it would soon be over, let alone rejoice at the prospect. All sense of joy had been tortured out of us.

We knew that now we had only a few miles left, yet every star had long been kindled in the sky before we reached the crossing place. There we left one sledge, and with Jørgensen on the other, well covered with our stiff-frozen sleeping-bags and warmed by the weakest of our dogs, Iversen and I flung ourselves into the traces and hauled, hauled for all we were worth, cracked our whips to get our few dogs to make a final spurt, inciting them with yells and cries that we hoped would also be heard by our companions out there in the darkness. Thus, on December 17, after fifteen days' toil from Danmarks Havn our eighty-six-day-long sledge journey finally ended; for suddenly, in the pitch dark night, with the aurora borealis flaming above our heads, the solid outline of the ship loomed in front of us like a section of denser night.

A light or two gleamed in the darkness; then we heard a dog howl and at that our poor brutes also understood that rest was near. They gave short joyful barks, such as we had not heard for a long time, pricked their ears and in joyful anticipation of all that now was within hearing and smelling distance, they picked up their tails and pulled as they had not pulled for a long time. They managed quite a speed, and with Iversen and I lumbering stiff-leggedly alongside in a weird kind of gallop we reached *Alabama*, while the others came hurrying to meet us with lanterns to light the last bit of the way of our seven-hundred-mile long journey through the darkness to Lamberts Land and back.

We stumbled aboard and down into the cabin, where glad companions thrust great mugs of scalding coffee into our hands and wonderful thick slices of white bread with mountains of butter. And meanwhile, the ice in our clothes melted. We dripped water, and pools formed under us. Then, to the others' amazement, we began to peel off our sledging clothes, layer after layer, and all as dirty and wet as a floorcloth fit to be thrown away.

Nor were our dogs forgotten in the joy of our homecoming; they were given as much as they could eat and more. Of the twenty-three fit dogs we had had harnessed to our sledges when we left the ship on September 26, only seven returned with us; the rest of the faithful creatures had died on the way of exhaustion, hunger and cold. A sledge dog's life is a harsh one.

However, we did not think of that in our overwhelming joy at having got back; perhaps, too, we had grieved enough over each dog as it fell. So we stretched out in our warm, dry bunks, enjoying the security and the rest, and so we fell asleep in the delicious knowledge that it would be the same the next day. By the side of my bunk my faithful Girly lay and licked my hand; it was very largely due to her that we had not fared even worse.

We had got back at least, and the hardships of the journey were almost forgotten the moment we were sitting there with our mugs of scalding coffee, and completely forgotten when we had changed into dry things. And then — in a week it would be Christmas; in only four days' time the sun would stop gliding towards the south and start coming back to us, putting the fearful darkness to flight, bathing land and ice in its sunlight, thus enabling us to see where we were treading and making sledging a joy.

Thus there was plenty to be joyful about that first night in the safe shelter of *Alabama*.

CHAPTER IV

Goodbye to Ship and Comrades

Five men on the inland ice — Farwell party —
Jørgensen and Unger in Alabama *— A friend's gift*

It was a sparkling clear day in April 1910 and the inland ice stretched
as far as the eye could see, a glittering white surface that was only
broken here and there by blue ice hummocks that attracted the sun's
rays and reflected them as shafts of compressed light which ignited
the wealth of coarse-grained ice crystals with which the bitter frost
had sprinkled the inland ice, making its harsh surface sparkle under
the caress of the sun.

To the north there was nothing but ice to be seen, ice and still more
ice; but to the south-west the black mountains in Queen Louise's Land
had burst through the white covering like mighty tussocks. In the
morning of Time they had been thrown up from the glowing interior
of the earth as roaring volcanoes and had slung red-hot lava high into
the air and sent great clouds of smoke swirling across the land that now
was covered by a cap of ice thousands of feet thick. To the south of us
this covering of ice was corrugated like sea frozen during a storm, and
it was across those hills and dales that, during the last fortnight, we had
hauled our heavy sledges from the sea ice, which we could still glimpse
far away in the south-east. How smooth it now looked in the distance,
but in reality it had been so uneven that we had often been on the point
of despair and wondered how we were ever to get through its labyrinth
of ice hills, pack ice and deep snow.

We could see the rash of islands and skerries in distant Dove Bay
looking like large black ships on a sea of white. It made a lovely sight
from up where we were, but when we had been down there among
them, the islands had towered above us, making our sledges like tiny

dinghies being urged across a rigid sea by sweating, shouting men, and the loose blowing snow like spume.

It was a desolate landscape, yet infinitely more alive than that across which we were now gazing. There, three thousand feet below and more than sixty miles away, those large black ships had been like milestones on our way to the mighty ice cap, which we had glimpsed between them and on which we now stood. Down there, we had been able to see signs of living creatures, the spade-like footprints of bears sauntering about the ice in the hope of sniffing out one of the seals that spend the winter snugly in snow caves above their breathing holes. There is nothing that appeals more to a hungry bear than the scent of seal, which sets it digging and leads it down to where a careful old mother seal or a newborn calf awaits it. Occasionally we saw the gory signs of such tragedies on the white snow.

Light-footed foxes followed in the shambling tracks of the sedate bear, living well on its leavings, both in the form of meat and what had been meat before it had passed through the bear. And high in the air above us ravens winged their way across the ice looking out for the meal that the great Provider had prepared for them.

There was life all right on the ice there far below us, but up here! . . . Not a living thing, not a track or a footprint apart from those we and our dogs had made; there was not even a bird to be seen in the clear, quivering heavens, not a sound to be heard. The inland ice is desolate; horribly, utterly desolate.

On this inland ice stood two small conical tents like dark toad-stools sprung from the white snow. Round the tents lay our dogs. Most were enjoying the rest and the sunshine after a hard stage, but one or two of the more enterprising were bustling about in vain hope of finding something edible we might have forgotten to stow away when we camped. Eagerly they sniffed the lovely smell of food from the sledges and would gladly have filched something, if only they could; but we were careful to see that they had no opportunity, and it was seldom they got anything out of their efforts other than a taste of the whip.

The dogs fought, as is the custom of dogs, especially when there are four bitches to every dog — a sad result of the arduous trip to Lamberts Land the previous winter which had lost us most of our strong dogs.

In a team of normal composition it is the male dogs that fight for the bitches' favours, with hair flying and blood flowing, but it was the other way round with us. Our bitches fought like furies for the fleeting attention of the dogs, which were less enduring even than usual, since there were other bitches humbly offering themselves or tearing and biting at the one momentarily enjoying a god's favours.

This circumstance had already caused us a lot of trouble and was to cause us plenty more. Luckily, the period of heat ought to be over soon, and we could expect a little peace to come to our pugnacious animals. And we hoped that they would also recover their strength, once the violent love-making was at an end.

These and other things we spoke of, as the five of us held a farewell party in one of the small tents up there on the inland ice. We had come so far together, but now our ways were to part. Laub, Bessel and Poulsen had come with us far enough, and we only hoped that we had left them with enough provisions to get back to our winter quarters at distant Shannon Island, and perhaps even to do a little exploring in that infinitude of mountain peaks which together go by the name of Queen Louise's Land.

Iversen and I, the other two of the five, had replenished our provisions from the returning party's load, so that our sledges were carrying all the weight they could stand and a little more than we could reasonably ask our dogs to haul. However, we could not dispense with an ounce of what we had, so somehow or other we would have to manage. We needed all the food we could possibly haul along with us, as we were going first to Danmarks Fjord and from there would try to make our way back to the ship along the coast, a journey of a thousand miles without counting the innumerable detours, unavoidable on such a journey, which unfortunately were bound to add at least a couple of hundred miles to the distance.

We drank some weak tea, greedily munched a biscuit or two and glared inhospitably when one of our three guests reached out for another. After that we demonstratively put the lid on the biscuit box and sat on it, while we set about deciding who was to have which dogs. We had by far the longest distance to go and had to have most of the dogs and the best, for at a pinch the others, who were returning to the ship, could pull the sledge themselves. That was as it should be and both parties were agreed, both we who were going the long way to Danmarks Fjord to search for the notes Mylius-Erichsen might possibly have left, and the three who relatively soon would again be enjoying all the edible delights *Alabama* had to offer.

It was a Spartan, but a very pleasant little feast. When we had divided up provisions and dogs to everyone's satisfaction, we got into our sleeping bags and lay there chatting: about the winter that now was past and almost forgotten, about the violent storms and the mighty fall of snow that had made outdoor work all but impossible; about the difficult dark period that had slightly cowed us all, despite the luxury of living on board, though we had joyful memories of the few fine still days with cloudless skies, twinkling stars, flaming northern lights, and so incredibly bright a moon that Iver had insisted it must be a hallucination, for no such moon existed. On those moonlit days it had been our joy to harness the dogs to an empty sledge and race across the ice on a hunt for bear or one of the musk oxen, which lived such a grim life in that snow-clad land that we told ourselves it must be easier for them to die than continue their search for food where no food was to be found. We spoke of the joy and the solemnity of that bitterly cold day in the middle of February, when the sun had come back to us after its three and a half months visit to the southern hemisphere. And we teased Iversen good-humouredly because, in a flush of enthusiasm at seeing the first sunbeam of the year kindle flashing glints in all the infinite numbers of ice crystals on ship and land, he had rushed about shouting: "Come and see, the sun is back, the sun is back," his voice ringing far out over the land.

Had he doubted that it would? Perhaps it would not be strange if he had, for you can scarcely take in the wonder of it, when the sun does at last return after being below the horizon for close on four months. You miss it dreadfully, as you miss its most faithful companion, shadow; you feel so strangely naked, so alone without your shadow. But the sun had come back and our shadows with it; black and so infinitely long that they almost seemed to reach the horizon in the north. We had run up on to the crest of the ridge to keep the sun in view as long as possible, and had stared southwards straight at its orange-coloured disc as it rolled along the horizon in a blaze of colours, so violent and so inharmonious in their fervour, as if it were a blaze kindled by demons wanting to burn the earth to cinders. Yet at the same time, high up in the zenith, the sky was of a dull blue colour, and in the north so black and grim that we had shivered at the sight of it.

For a few minutes the sun had delighted us, then it had disappeared again below the horizon. As it went, it was as though our shadows had run off towards the north and vanished or been obliterated. But the next day the sun had returned and brought light, colour and shadows, and life was good to live. And then the time for our long sledge journey was at hand.

We spoke, too, of the two others left at the ship, of Jørgensen who should have been with us on the inland ice, only his feet had been so badly frost-bitten on our way back from Lamberts Land that we had to amputate five toes — without a doctor, without antiseptics, without any better anaesthetic than half a bottle of whisky, a job none of us could think of without shuddering. Jørgensen had taken it like a man, and never once had we heard him complain about being thus debarred from taking part in the long sledge journeys we were to make in the spring. What he thought, we did not know, but he joked and laughed with us when there was anything to be amused at, and helped us in whatever way he could from his bunk. He was a man indeed, that Jørgensen, we were all agreed about that, and as we lay in our sleeping bags we elaborated the point in our attempts to find something to talk about and so be together a little while longer.

And there was that willing horse Unger, who undertook all the jobs no one else wanted to do. He so badly wanted to do the right thing, but as he did not know what was done and what was not done on board a ship, he often did the wrong thing. Now, as we were about to sever the last tie with the ship and our companions, we longingly thought of the wonderful dinner he had made for us the last evening on board, and how he must have worked all night to have produced the magnificent breakfast he served us before we set out. When we had finished it and gulped down a mug of his scalding coffee, we went out on to the ice and to the sledges to which the dogs had long been harnessed, disentangled the traces and set out on our way, but not without thanking Unger, the good companion, for the help he had always given so willingly, and for all the good meals he had made us at a time when meals were the only bright spots in our day.

It was not very easy to say goodbye to each other in that desolation of ice. Under what conditions would we meet again? The future was utterly uncertain, for so much could happen both to them and to us. Thus, we put off the moment as long as possible, sipping our hot tea and racking our brains for something else to say.

We were all of us a little uneasy, and when the position of the sun in the sky showed that we had procrastinated a little too long already, we said "goodbye and thanks for everything" and went our separate ways.

Our three companions headed south and soon disappeared among the hummocks on the uneven inland ice, leaving Iversen and me alone on that great white waste. Whatever happened now, we must rely solely on ourselves and what we carried on our sledges.

When our day's work was finished and we were preparing to creep into our sleeping bags, I found under mine the exact number of biscuits and amount of butter that we had sacrificed on the farewell feast. "Sacrificed" is not too big a word, for under such conditions biscuits were infinitely precious, and butter too. On the biscuits lay a piece of paper on which was written: "You two need this more than we three. Good journey and safe return. Laub, Bessel and Poulsen."

Iversen and I sat and looked at the piece of paper, at the biscuits — I think there were six — and at the butter, and at each other. The gift was like a last handclasp from our faithful, considerate friends.

CHAPTER V

Alone between Heaven and Earth

*Crevasses in the inland ice — A lure for the dogs — Unsafe surface —
Storm and drifting snow — Frost-bite — Stormy days*

Iversen and I stood on a hummock of ice and watched our companions
till they were out of sight. Soon they had disappeared down a valley of
ice and when, after waiting, we did not see them reappear on the next
ridge, we realized that they had found a practicable way behind it and
had been engulfed in that great ice sea. Then we nodded to each other,
and, without saying much, quietly got on with the job of reloading our
sledges, dividing our gear and provisions between them in such a way
that if we lost a sledge in one of the many crevasses with which we were
perpetually surrounded, and whose black mouths led to an underworld
whence escape was impossible, we would have at least a theoretical
chance of managing for a while with what remained on the other sledge.

Knowing what had to be done, there was little need for words and
so we said less and less and in the end fell silent. Neither of us liked the
silence, though, especially Iver, and after one lengthy pause I heard him
muttering some words to himself over and over again. Finally he found
the tune, and that was as peculiar as the words:

"Alone, alone, quite alone between Heaven and earth,
Alone with dogs and ice, alone, quite alone."

Louder and louder grew his mumble, till finally he burst into song.
He glanced sideways at me, and I nodded in time to his improvised
ditty, that sounded so melancholy and yet was so heartening in that
great deathly silent waste.

He was a good comrade, Iver; the sort of man with whom you could go on a really long journey, such as that on which we were starting, for we had a thousand miles ahead of us, every foot of which we must cover before we got back to *Alabama*. By that time the grip of winter would be broken and summer have come; each mountain-side would be agush with streams, each hollow a gleaming mirror of water with migrant birds from the fair South disporting themselves on it.

First we had to cover the 270 miles across the inland ice to Danmarks Fjord, and that would be the hardest leg of the journey. The immense ice cap extended far and wide all round us, thousands of feet thick and nearly five thousand where we were. To the west stretched line after line of ice hills up to Greenland's spine, where the mass of ice reached a thickness of close on ten thousand feet. From north to south this armour of ice is some 2300 miles long, and from east to west nearly 500 miles wide on the average — nearly one and a quarter million square miles, two and a half million cubic miles of ice! This inconceivable mass of ice has accumulated through the ages on a country that once, in the morning of Time, was covered with luxuriant tropical vegetation.

The two of us, then, were alone on all that ice — apart from our three companions who had disappeared beyond the ice horizon a few hours before. We were as cut off from the world's seething mass of humanity, as if in some miraculous way we had been flung out into space and had landed in the largest crater on the moon, surrounded by an unbroken ring-wall of inconceivably high mountains across which no way led to the equally desolate territory beyond.

It was in truth a dismal place to find yourself in, no place for a man to be.

But what was the matter with us? Why were we complaining now that at last we had got where we had so long hankered to be? We had no reason to be disgruntled, quite the reverse. We had come there voluntarily, although perhaps rashly; we had even looked forward to getting up on to the great ice cap which we regarded as a more or less practicable road to our goal.

Nevertheless, we were slightly bewildered at finding ourselves alone up there on that boundless waste, where never a bird winged its way between sky and ice, where the scanning eye could not discover even the smallest track of roaming animal, where there were no other insects than the fleas our dogs carried in their thick hair, if even they had not been frozen to death. Even a miserable worm was too sensible to go where we had ventured of our own free will.

It was a dangerous wilderness, in that so many things both unforseen and unavoidable might happen, things which would mean death to us both and to the dogs and the fleas that perhaps still bred on them, sucking the blood of their weakened hosts. These might be quite minor things, a sprained ankle for example, that anywhere else would be worth no more than a regretful shrug of the shoulders. Elsewhere in the world of men a sprain was an easy thing to cure, but here it was a mortal hurt, not only for the one who suffered the injury, but also for his companion who would have to wait till the other had recovered and could put his weight on that foot before he could continue. There was nothing we could do, if one of us met with the least accident; there was no help to be had, however badly we needed it, no refuge to be found: either we both got through, or we both died and became as stiff and frozen as everything else around us.

Those were things you must not think too much about; thinking did not help and only tended to destroy your peace of mind. There we were on the inland ice, two rash humans who had gone there voluntarily, and what we had to do was to get down again as quickly as we could — on the other side. Nor had we any time to waste, so we harnessed the dogs to the sledges, took a last look at the site of our camp to make doubly sure that nothing had been forgotten, cracked our long whips at the dogs, hitting them where they felt it most, and flung ourselves into the traces to get the sledges going and so that the dogs should under-stand that the time for idling was over, and that now it was a question of pulling and pulling hard. So, with a great commotion of howls and cries that was good to hear in that eerie silence, we laboriously got under way, taking the first of our lonely steps towards the land round the first arm of Danmarks Fjord, 270 miles away. We hoped that when we had got there, we should find not too breakneck a way down the tall steep wall of ice, probably more than three hundred feet high, which bounded the ice cap in the north, and so escape from that hell of ice, cold and paralysing stillness.

We had long since acquired due respect for the many crevasses and fissures that gaped dangerously all round us. Some were narrow, others several yards wide, anything up to a hundred feet or more. Often they were hidden beneath a covering of hard wind-pressed snow, so that we never saw them, but merely felt them as the middle of the snow bridge gave slightly; or there might be a sudden, eerie, hollow sound as you thrust your feet in hard to keep the sledge going and happened to be over such a chasm.

Mostly the snow bridges held, but it did happen and not so seldom, that one broke beneath our weight or that of the sledge, and for minutes, sometimes scores of minutes, it was touch and go whether or not we got across with the dogs, sledges, gear and ourselves safe and sound.

We were lucky, and each time a snow bridge broke, there was always some insignificant little protruberance in the steep, often vertical lip of glass-hard ice that stopped the slipping sledge from falling into unfathomable depths, so that we were able, with infinite caution, to remove its precious load and carry it to safe ice, then draw the sledge to safety from the crevasse that was blue-white and gleaming up by the surface, but black, black as the grave some few yards down towards its icy depths. Once, however, a trace broke and a wretched dog fell in. It fell and fell and fell. We never heard it strike bottom, never heard so much as a whimper from the poor brute, which perhaps fell so far that no sound could reach up to the surface where Iver and I stood looking at each other, aghast at the thought that either of us, or both, might just as easily have been sent hurtling into those depths, through the glassy jaws of ice down into the blue-blackness.

One day when we thought we were relatively safe from crevasses, for fortunately there were such days as well, I heard Iver call out suddenly.

I did not catch what he said, but the fright and horror in his voice were all too obvious. I spun round to see what had happened and saw Iver lying flat on the ice beside a black hole in the snow calling: "Puppy, Puppy, don't you hear me?"

In a couple of bounds I reached the hole from which the searing breath of the ice struck at our faces. Iver gave me a horrified look and said:

"Puppy's trace broke, he's down there," and he nodded down towards the black depths. "I didn't hear him strike on the side or bottom, so perhaps he hasn't even reached it yet. When we stopped for a rest a while ago, he crawled up on to the sledge, snuggled into me and gazed at me with his faithful eyes."

A bead of ice rolled down Iver's cheek into his beard, where it froze fast; another followed, then another, a whole lot; but five minutes later we were on our way north again, heading for other crevasses, broad or narrow as fate decreed, easy to cross or only to be negotiated after a long search for a snow bridge to which we dared entrust our weight.

There were days when our feet went through the fragile bridges however careful we were, however cautiously we tested their strength before venturing out on to them; and there were other days when it felt as though a kindly fate were guiding our steps, and we became more and more reckless, crossing snow bridges without first testing them and smiling superior smiles when we heard the ominous, hollow sound beneath our feet, though we would be careful to step but lightly on the snow and swing our whips furiously over the dogs, for the sledges had to be kept moving. To halt meant falling, and death.

I always kept a small lump of pemmican handy, and this I produced whenever we had to cross a specially unpleasant snow bridge, one that sagged in the middle and yet seemed safe enough, if only we could keep the sledges moving. The dogs were shown it and allowed to snuff in the delicious smell of it. They would howl and bark in their eagerness to get so rare a titbit, leap forward in the traces to get going and when they were all strained to the utmost, to their annoyance they would see the desired pemmican slung far ahead of them to the other side of the chasm. Now, it was a case of who could get there first; and with tails waving in the joys of anticipation, tongues hanging far out, and flanks going like bellows, the dogs would pull like creatures possessed in the hope of being the first to reach the titbit on the other side, the titbit they never got. They never got it, because I was always first across the bridge and kicked the lump of pemmican far out of their reach; then I picked it up to use it again in the next emergency, while the dogs flew at each other, biting and yelping, each believing that the other had had the luck to snap up what was safely back in my pocket. I used the same lump throughout the whole journey across that waste of ice.

It was swindling, if you like, and a shame on the trusting dogs who never suspected that we humans could be so mean, but I had to be mean, in order to get them and the sledge across those especially dangerous places.

We came across long stretches where the surface ice was splintered like a piece of glass that has been struck by a ricocheting bullet, riven by long narrow crevasses, not broad enough to fall down and perhaps not dangerous to us or the dogs and sledges, yet most unpleasant to tread in, for, if your luck were out, you could break your leg on the sharp edge of the ice, or sprain an ankle. That was a thing of which we were very afraid, as the chances of it happening were considerable, but we just had to disregard them. If we worried about everything that could have happened to us we might just as well have stayed at home in Copenhagen. We toiled on across the splintered ice, treading into fissures with one leg or perhaps with both, but getting up and out again before we had time to realize what had happened, and just flinging the word *fissure* over our shoulders to our companion following with his sledge a short way behind.

Of course, I always went in the lead, as was only right, and one day when we were crossing a part where there were unusually many of these narrow crevasses, I heard Iversen start chuckling away to himself. I turned in amazement and some irritation to see what could be the cause of all this merriment, for which I could see no occasion at all. "What are you laughing at?" I asked.

"What?" Iversen replied and laughed aloud. "Because you remind me of a toy I had as a child and used to love, a Jack-in-the-box, I think it was called. Anyway, you're exactly like the Jack who shot out of the box every time I eased the lid. You are just as black as he was; your hair is long and tufted like his, and sticks out in the same way. And you flap your arms, just as he did as he popped out of the box. You're down one moment, so that I can scarcely see you, and up the next. In fact, you look fearfully funny."

It was all very well to talk of Jack-in-the-boxes and laugh at me, but it was my shins I was cutting on the sharp ice, and I would be the one whom fate perhaps would thrust down into some box, so that I stayed there. I certainly could see nothing to laugh at.

Up there on the inland ice, when the days were golden with sunlight and the frost so hard that the mercury had frozen in the thermometer, and the paraffin become so thick that it had to be thawed a bit in the warmth of our sleeping bags, before we could get it to burn in the Primus or even flow out of the can, there often happened something that was really lovely. All at once we would hear a faint rustling all round us, like the frou-frou of heavy silk, and at that moment every one of the infinite number of snow and ice crystals on the surface suddenly shone and gleamed most colourfully, as though each had been a sparkling diamond. It looked lovely and for an instant created an illusion of life around us; but it also got on our nerves and made us start each time it happened and think for a moment that we had come unawares onto a fragile snow bridge, which just then was breaking beneath us. The dogs were as nervy as we were and leaped on stiff legs as high as the traces let them, barked, howled and whined with fear.

In the end, however, we discovered why the dead white surface of the inland ice could become so lovely: it was due to the hard-frozen crust of snow breaking beneath the weight of the sledge and sinking a centimeter or so into the softer snow beneath. Knowing that, our fright was only momentary, and the next moment we were swinging our whips over the terrified dogs and shouting ourselves hoarse: "Silly brutes. There's no danger of crevasses here. Pull, pull, damn you!"

All of us who had gone up there were silly, both men and dogs.

We were sitting on our sledges in a dip full of crevasses, having a breather after an especially hard stage, when Iver asked one of his innumerable questions: "Tell me, what makes the crevasses? Why are there many in one place and none in another?"

Iver pondered problems as he trudged along by the side of his sledge, pulling as much as all his dogs together. His was an alert mind, and he saw and noted a great deal. Everything was new to him, who previously had spent his days in a workshop or a ship's engine room. He wanted to know about everything that interested him in the cold white hell up there; and when the labour of forcing the sledge along was not enough to shut his mouth, he asked questions interminably, thinking that I had ready answers for all that could happen on the ice, that I knew everything about crevasses, dogs, sledging, weather and all the other things that can interest those who travel by sledge. It was flattering, as long as I could think of a plausible answer, but excessively irritating when I was tired or could not supply an answer that perhaps I should have known. Usually such bouts of questioning ended with a gruff: "Oh, shut up, Iver. Save your breath for pulling to help the dogs."

Then the good Iver would sulk for a bit and look as though he would never open his mouth again. But all resentment vanished as soon as the crevasses were again gaping at us from all sides with their blue-black jaws. They were both dangerous and a waste of time, yet one way or another we were always able to make our way through those labyrinths of cracks and fissures, large and small; but progress was slow, often all too slow for us, who saw our provisions sinking day by day without our being able to cover the necessary distance. At some stage or other of our journey we were going to have to pay for all the time lost because of the crevasses.

Unpleasant and time-consuming as the crevasses were, our worst enemy on the inland ice was nevertheless the searing, biting wind. It almost always blew in our faces, driving snow in front of it in dense clouds. The granules of snow stung us like swarms of impertinent insects, until incipient frost-bite made noses, cheeks, ears and fingers insensitive to their attack. Then we had to remove our warm mittens and use our hands to thaw out our faces, rubbing them with snow so sharp and hard-frozen that it acted like sand-paper and rubbed holes in our insensitive skin. The snow melted in our bare hands, so that icy water ran over our fingers that were themselves already threatened, and quickly they too became white, insensitive and dead, and had to be rubbed in their turn, till the blood tingled and the pain became all but unbearable. That melted more snow, sent more water running over our hands to freeze and cake on the fur where our sleeves closely encircled our wrists. It was a vicious circle and very difficult to escape from.

We had always to be on the lookout for signs of frost-bite in each other's faces, the waxen-yellow patch that spreads so swiftly, if it is not halted in time. As a rule frost-bite is not immediately noticed by the one affected, and thus, when the weather was so cold that frost-bite was likely as was almost always the case on the inland ice, we had to keep a sharp watch on each other. As soon as I saw a dead white patch on Iver's face, I gave warning: "Iver, thaw your nose, it's frozen." Often the reply when he looked up and saw my face, was a curt: "Yours too." So then we had to halt and rub till the blood was circulating again and ears or nose had begun to tingle and burn, instead of being dead and insensitive.

Swirling snow, borne along by the howling wind, swept the loose snow off the inland ice and pelted us with it, till it filled our beards and caked there, pressing up towards our noses so that we had to scratch it away. Eyebrows and eyelashes became hung with garlands of tiny icicles, which we were continually having to rub away in order to see at all. The driving snow found every hole, every opening however small, in our warm skins and caked on our shirts and underclothes; there the heat of our bodies melted it, so that it dripped and ran where water should not be, where it would have been unpleasant in any circumstances, but in ours was insufferable.

We had a bad time of it on the inland ice, but our poor dogs were even worse off, for they suffered from the low driving snow much more than we. Often we were able to stride along against a hard wind with the upper part of our bodies in lovely sunshine, so that we looked out across a billowing sea of wind-borne snow in which our dogs were submerged. Under such conditions it was almost impossible to keep going.

But we had to get forward, and forward we got, though only slowly, for nothing takes the stuffing out of dogs like driving snow. We had to keep urging the wretched animals on, in order to get the most out of an impossible day. And we were loath to use our whips, perhaps not so much out of consideration for the dogs, as for ourselves, for the wind often flung the long lash back at us; and it had a strange propensity to catch us in the face, just where there was no fur or beard to protect the skin, and its sharp frozen edge drew blood. The dog whip is a double-edged weapon that castigates dogs and men indiscriminately. Thus, if there was a head wind, we urged on the dogs with cries and shouts and curses, but we might just as well have saved our breath, as they had no effect at all without an accompanying crack of the whip. It was no wonder, either, that the dogs struck and neither could nor would work when the wind was against them; for their panting breath melted the snow driving round their heads, so that it settled in lumps of ice on their poor faces, freezing to the hair, especially round their eyes, so that they could not see.

We were continually having to clear the ice and snow off the leader-dogs' eyes, for if they could not see where they were treading, the whole team must halt. The other dogs could stumble blindly across the ice; theirs was just to haul and pull; they needed only to follow the leader-dog, who anyway would see to it that they did. Each time we halted for a breather or to gather strength for the next tussle or to clean the dogs' eyes or whatever else the reason, the dogs would creep behind the sledges to get out of the searing wind and the stabbing snow. That always caused a commotion: the dogs bit and tore at each other to get the best places close to the shelter of the sledge, and within a few minutes the traces would be tangled and, glassy with frozen saliva and urine, turned into a hard, frozen mass of knots, almost impossible to disentangle. So, before we could get going again, that tangle had to be thawed and undone, sometimes using our teeth, but always our bare hands, which became white and stiff — frost-bite again.

It was a bitter business sledging into a stiff wind and driving snow, but it had to be blowing very hard before we gave up and stopped and made camp. When we halted, the dogs could rest at once, digging holes for themselves and letting their bitter enemy, the wind, cover them with a warm coverlet of snow. Then they were relatively comfortable, but we had a horrible time getting the tent pitched in the furious gusts that almost always heralded a storm. All loose objects, especially anything edible, had to be taken into the tent, and often we had several hours drudgery in biting cold and furious wind, before we ourselves could crawl into the relative warmth and shelter of the tent. But before we could relax, we must quickly restore the circulation to those places on face, hands and perhaps toes as well, where frost-bite had started.

The days when the wind came storming off the inland ice and forced us to take shelter were indeed hard for both us and the dogs. It would be a long time even after we had got inside the tent, before we got sufficient warmth into our bodies, especially our fingers, to be able to handle the Primus. How lovely that Primus was when it was burning with a warm, blue-yellow flame, but how searingly cold before it was lit, when to touch it with bare fingers was like grasping red-hot iron.

Everything was accomplished in time, however; then, the dogs fed, the tent in order and the reindeer hair linings of our sleeping bags more or less thawed, we would ease ourselves into them and stretch our stiff limbs, enjoy our pemmican and the rest, and then fall asleep in the hope that perhaps the weather would be good in the morning.

Hope we always had, though it was mostly deceived, and angrily we would creep deeper into the clammy warmth of our sleeping bags, when we woke to another day and heard the wind whistling, howling and roaring round us, heard the smacks as heavy lumps of frozen snow struck the walls of the tent that sagged beneath the weight of the snow and the press of the wind, so that the little shelter we had made against storm and snow was even smaller than before.

It would not have been so miserable if we could have stayed in our sleeping bags and "enjoyed" life; but however bad the weather was, we had to go out. In the first place we had to take a look at the weather and see if there were any signs of improvement and any likelihood of our being able to sledge on, which was regrettably seldom the case. The dogs also had to be seen to; each had to be hounded, wildly protesting, from its warm den, to prevent it being suffocated by the thickening layer of snow; and also they had to be fed. They were not given much, for days of compulsory rest were wasted as far as distance was concerned, and we could not afford to give the dogs more than would just relieve the worst of their hunger. Food was precious and had to be eked out most carefully.

The same strict rule applied, of course, to us in the tent, and on lay days hunger gnawed at the stomachs of both men and dogs. Abstinence, voluntary or compulsory, was required, if we were to be able to complete our long journey; yet on the other hand neither dogs nor men could be allowed to go so hungry that it weakened them. It was not easy to decide how much was necessary, especially when you yourself were ravening.

One idle day was not so unwelcome, for there was always a lot of mending of skins and footgear to be done. And then there was the journal to be written up on paper so cold that your breath turned to ice as it touched the relatively white sheet, which it inevitably brushed. We had to watch out for this, for once or twice we had discovered to our annoyance that the account of the previous day's happenings, which we had written so laboriously with cold, stiff fingers, had been written on nothing more permanent than a thin film of ice, which melted if the temperature in the tent rose slightly, or if we stroked a relatively warm hand across the paper. And with the film of ice the writing also vanished, and it was all to be done again, after first drying and warming the paper.

We spent much time measuring distances on the map and putting dots where we were, and in comparing our progress with the timetable I had worked out in my warm cabin in *Alabama:* to which we had to keep if our food were to last. We dared not rely on finding game where the three who had perished had found none.

The result of the balance we struck was not very encouraging, and we realized, while we were still on the inland ice, that the day must come when we would find ourselves without provisions on the desolate coast far north of our winter quarters, which we would then not be able to reach unless we could find game. And the thought of game, the word *game*, was so inspiring, that we could never quite rid ourselves of the hope of encountering something to shoot. We talked about it endlessly, this question which might be one of life or death, trying to see it from every side — and there was plenty of time to do so during the long days when the weather was stormy. And we always came to the comforting conclusion that of course we could not help finding game once we got to proper land and the coast, that there we must come across animals as we sledged along. We revelled in thinking and talking of all the meat we were going to have, looked forward to it and drove the warning voice of doubt from our minds; we talked of the musk oxen we could not help hitting, of the bears our bullets would kill, and of the seals we should find dozing in the sunshine or on an ice-floe, secure in the consciousness that no danger could threaten them.

These were encouraging thoughts and often they had to take the place of a meal, which they *could* do — for a time at least. So while the storm howled round the tent and the snow swirled madly, we talked gaily of how the dogs would enjoy it, when at last they were able once more to gorge on all the juicy meat there would be lying about at the end of a successful hunt on the ice.

CHAPTER VI

Still on the Inland Ice

Talking of dogs — Worries about provisions — Melancholy prospects

Many hours of the gloomy tedious lay days of enforced idleness were spent in talk of our dogs. They were always in our thoughts and one or more nearly always in view, for my leader-dog, Girly, who was staid and more or less house-trained, was usually in our tent and often lying on top of our sleeping bags, where she acted as a live hot-water bottle and helped to warm our feet.

Girly loved being with us. She lay quietly in the little tent following our every movement with her lovely faithful eyes, giving a little happy squeak at each kind word we gave her, and whining with delight when she was given a microscopic piece of our food. Girly was a handsome dog. She was a great help on the laborious days of sledging, and as a tent fellow she helped to cheer us up during the irksome tedium of the lay days.

Iver hated it that my leader-dog had a permanent place in the tent, while his leader-dog, Bjørn, which he thought every bit as good, had to suffer the hardships of living outside. Bjørn was of the same opinion and squeezed as close as he could to the wall of the tent, so as to share in what took place on the other side of the thin cloth. He gave a squeak when he heard Girly squeak, whined when he heard her joyful bark at being given some tiny titbit. And each time there was this chorusing on either side of the tent wall, Iver would look at me reproachfully: "Did you hear that? It really did sound as though that good Bjørn was glad of Girly's living in luxury here with us. Shouldn't we . . . ?" And he would look at me interrogatively, and I would nod agreement.

The next moment Iver would be out of his sleeping bag and of course he could not avoid touching the tent cloth. That sent the hoar frost sprinkling down over us, into our hair and beards, trickling down our necks and reaching far down chest and back before it melted, falling thick on the sleeping bags and turning into icy water. But Iver never thought of that, nor of the storm of snow that swept in when he opened the door of the tent; "Come along, Bjørn, but you must behave," he added hesitantly, "or the boss will be angry."

Bjørn did not need to be invited twice; he came in like an avalanche. Bjørn was a big dog. His fur and tail were full of snow and he expressed his boundless joy at being let in by violent, ingratiating wrigglings of his body that sent the snow swirling round the tent. He was an awkward friend to invite in. But Iver was happy and tried to mitigate the violence of Bjørn's delight; Bjørn and Girly were happy too, and, of course, tried to romp. As a rule Iver would have a tiny piece of pemmican that he had been keeping for his pet, who would whine with joy when he got it, while Girly came to me for comfort and solace. Then all would be cosy until the exuberant Bjørn, in his attempts at self-effacement, knocked the Primus over with his large bushy tail. That frightened him, and he tried to make amends by backing away from the disgusting cold thing, and in doing so stepped into our jug and knocked that over, then peed with fright at the damage he had done and at what he knew would be the inevitable result: expulsion from paradise into the cold and swirling snowstorm. And while Iver busied himself restoring order, he comforted himself by assuring me that one day Bjørn would learn how to behave in the tent, so that he could always be inside with us.

But Bjørn never did. Neither he nor Iver learned from experience, and every time we had Bjørn in the tent the unexpected always happened.

Even with half rations for men and dogs these days of enforced rest cost us some thirty pounds a day, which was a dreadful tax on our store of provisions when there was no mileage covered to counterbalance it. When we had nothing else to do in the tent, we reviewed our various dogs' capabilities so as to decide which did least for its food, and thus ought to be killed so that the others could live. Unfortunately, there were few of whom we could find anything good to say, and while the storm howled round us, we spent hours deciding which dog we could best do without, which shirked its work most and really should long since have paid with its life for its lack of interest in what is the sledge-dog's only justification: to haul, haul and go on hauling till it can haul no more.

As a rule, a good storm on the inland ice lasted a couple of days and nights, though one went on for five. When the weather forced us to lie idle for particularly long, the sentence of death we had passed would be carried out. Both of us would go out into the storm. The dogs would whine expectantly; and the wily Grimrian would literally tread on my heels in his efforts not to be seen, apparently knowing what it meant when I had a rifle in my hand. Then we would dig the condemned dog out of its warm snow-lair, press the muzzle of the rifle to its head, and it would die as the report rang out, without a gasp or a kick.

The report always set all the dogs howling in a lengthy concert, for they knew that now they were going to get warm meat to eat. Then, while the frost bit at our faces and fingers, we would skin the dead dog, cut it up and give each live dog its share, which was little enough, for up there on the inland ice the dogs had grown so wretchedly thin that there was little on them; yet it was enough to keep the survivors going for another day or two of storm without suffering too greatly from hunger.

We always took two pieces of the best meat back to the tent for Girly and Bjørn, so that they could feast on the remains of a companion who had been weighed and found wanting.

Bjørn always gobbled up his bit with delighted grunts and much smacking of his lips, but Girly would just smell hers, turn it over and smell the other side, take a cautious trial nibble at it — and then turn away from it and give me a most expressive look. If she had been able to talk, she would undoubtedly have said in a tone of reproach: "So all my hard work is rewarded with a piece of nauseous meat from a companion. How can you!" That was all very well, but what else could I do?

Bjørn would be keeping an eye on Girly, and when he saw that she was leaving the meat, he would approach cautiously; but Girly would not even protest when, warily and with his bad conscience showing in his eyes, he patted the lump to him with a paw and swallowed it in a

couple of gulps. Bjørn did not possess the finer feelings and was not one
to despise any food.

Iver and I would look at each other, always rather guiltily. Once I
patted Girly, petting her a bit because she was a good dog who refused
to eat a comrade; and, though I did not say anything, I may have smiled
a little exultingly at Iver. Anyway, he took it as a tacit condemnation of
Bjørn, who had not such fine feelings, and suddenly squeezing out of
his warm damp sleeping bag, he opened the door of the tent and thrust
the yelping Bjørn into the raging storm and cold snow, without Bjørn
having any idea what he had done: "Damned cannibal," Iver shouted at
him. "Enjoy yourself there!"

Then Girly was given a microscopic piece of an almost invisible bit
of pemmican as a reward for virtue.

Those days of storm were long and difficult to get through. We spent
forty-nine days on the inland ice and of these we were stormbound for
nineteen whole days, and various half days. That was a fearful lot.

That did not exhaust the devilry of the weather, for calm fine days
were so rare there that we had eighteen days (other than stormbound
ones) of slow, laborious battling against a more or less violent wind,
before we had our first good day.

I must admit that we were making our journey too early. In the
summer, or early summer, the weather is much better; or so one is led
to believe. I had always known that we were starting out too early, but I
had no choice: either we had to cross the inland ice as early as we possibly could, or we must be prepared to spend the summer somewhere or
other on the coast, which would involve another wintering, and for that
we had no great desire.

I had chosen to sledge early across the inland ice in the hope that
the powers which govern wind and weather would be gracious. They
were, in fact, the reverse, so that, though we had chosen almost the
worst time for the inland ice, where storm was the rule, we still had to
be prepared to spend the summer somewhere on the coast. And if our
rifles could not get us food there, what then? There would be no more
"and then?" Mylius-Erichsen and his companions had not survived,

though one of them was a Greenlander, accustomed to keeping alive in that harsh land.

We had had a hard time of it with the dirty weather and, in all probability, would have just as bad a time with hunger during the summer. Which of the two would be worse, was a matter of opinion; both situations were grim and could cost us our lives. Now we had come through the storms: would we do as much with the hunger?

We had every excuse to consider the outlook dark. The provisions we carried had been too few for the consumption necessitated by the days of storm and no progress, and it was obvious long before we came down off the inland ice that we must make up our minds to spend the summer there, as it was only in the autumn we could hope to get back to *Alabama*. Those nineteen days of storm would cost us a whole year, at least a year — if we even came through the summer.

CHAPTER VII

Last Days on the Inland Ice

Ice and cold improve — Land straight ahead — The dogs break into the tent — Run-away ride — A fairy world — Back on land

Luckily, it could also happen that when we woke, we would sit up in surprise in our sleeping bags, listening for the sound we were accustomed to hear, listening intently without catching the least hiss of snow against the tent; and if, at the same time, the sun happened to be shining through the tent-cloth, filling with golden sunlight the little space the storms made so dreary, then we would be out of our sleeping bags in a flash and, while one made tea, the other hurried out on to the gaily lit inland ice, joyfully sniffed the fresh air, shuddered a little with the cold and set about getting all ready for the earliest possible start.

That could be a cold job when the temperature was so low that the mercury was frozen, and it became an even colder one when one day I remembered how, in Alaska, the Eskimos often ice the runners of their sledges when they want to drive quickly across snow that is free from stones. That was a thing we also should be able to do, and there was certainly no need to be afraid of stones ripping the ice off the runners, when we were on top of a layer of ice nearly 5,000 feet thick! So we tried icing our runners, and the experiment was a magnificent success — the sledges slid along almost on their own.

The dogs were highly surprised when we moved off and they found that they could scarcely feel the weight of the sledges. They barked loudly in amazement and turned round to see whether they had lost the sledge, or why they could no longer feel it. Then they saw our smiling faces and heard our words of encouragement "Keep going, little dogs. The sledges are there and will follow you all right."

And so they dashed ahead. Iver and I smiled to each other. It was almost incredible how easily everything went. The sun was shining, there was no wind to hamper us and we were maintaining a relatively good speed — praise be! There was, though, one nasty snake in our paradise: icing sledge runners in a temperature of thirty or forty degrees (Centigrade) below zero, perhaps even fifty, was a job for experts. We had filled our mouths with water to warm it slightly, then spat it out onto the runners and rubbed it with our bare hands along the wood, laying layer upon layer until the skin of ice was almost a millimetre thick. That was a cold job for bare fingers, and when at last we were done we discovered that our hands had been so numb, that we had never even noticed the big splinters of wood we had rammed into our palms.

We did not worry much about that, though. We could always pull the splinters out when the frost had gone from our hands. All that we were concerned with was to get the sledges gliding easily, so as to save the dogs' strength and cover as great a distance as possible, and thus make up some of the time we had lost.

The sledges did at least slip along easily on their iced runners, and once we had got so far north that the inland ice began to shelve down towards the land round Danmarks Fjord, sledging became a real joy instead of the inhuman toil it had been.

It was nearly May and the sun was high in the sky both at midnight and at noon. The worst of the crevasses and fissures were evidently behind us, for we saw but few of them, and a large mass of mountains was heaving itself up above the horizon far away in the north, more mountains to take the place of those we had struggled so hard to reach and pass.

The weather, too, had improved. There were not so many storms, and they neither so violent nor of such long duration as they had been. Obviously, we had the worst behind us. So, as we sped across the waste of ice, we urged the dogs on with fair promises of land and musk oxen, of such gorging as their bellies had never known before.

We called gay flippancies across to each other, as we strode along with sail on the sledge, for now we had a following wind instead of the interminable head wind that had blown till then. The tent, hoist on a mast of three skis lashed together, made a peculiar looking sail, but it served its purpose, increased our speed and enhanced our joy at the progress we were making. And, as usual, when things weren't going at all right with us, Iver sang most loudly; thus, across the inland ice, rang the comforting refrain:

> "Why should we sorrow,
> Why let things annoy?
> The world's not worth it
> 'Twas made for joy."

We certainly had no cause for tears. Fate had given us a warning rap over the fingers and had taught us to be less arrogant and sure of ourselves. We realized, of course, that we should have to spend the summer on the coast; but that all lay in the future, so why lament now when everything was going so well? So I just cracked my whip in time to Iver's song. This was the old Iver that I knew. But, Iver, do you not see the cirrus clouds coming up from the north, as though they were the long arm of the Ice King stretching out to catch us and keep us up there? They perhaps mean storm tomorrow, and you won't sing then. Then the wind will be whistling and howling its harsh song of wasted days and short commons, while the snow flakes whirl in their ghostly dance!

But Iver just laughed. "What of it," said he — "things are going well today, so why wail about possible disasters tomorrow. Perhaps there will be a storm, perhaps there won't; let us rejoice in the present, even if tomorrow stifles us."

There was something in that.

The sledging continued to go well — better and better, in fact, as the days came and went. The ominous cirrus clouds that till then had been such infallible harbingers of calamity now seemed to have lost contact with the future and the evils it had in store, and we stopped paying heed to them. Then, one day we at last saw the sight to which we had been looking forward so hugely; ahead and far below us we glimpsed land, land that was almost clear of snow, an incredible sight.

We left the sledges and dogs and walked on closer to the edge of the ice to see if there was a practicable way down to our promised land. For the first time for ages we had rifles bumping on our backs, and each bump was like the greeting of a good friend, one who might be able to procure us food; if only we could get down to the land of promise where game and meat — fantastic thought — were perhaps to be had.

However, when we reached the edge of the inland ice after some hours' walking, there was a sheer glacier wall of over 300 feet, down which it would have been impossible to lower the sledges, so we turned and walked back to our camp, fagged, disappointed and hungry. How near was our object, land, and yet how far.

The state in which we found the camp did nothing to improve our humour. The dogs, forgetting all their training as their masters walked off across the ice, had broken into the tent — nothing difficult about that — opened the tin boxes and eaten some of our precious provisions. The few miscreants had gobbled up over two stone of pemmican, plus a quantity of biscuits and some dried vegetables. The omniverous creatures had topped this off with a bit of sleeping bag, and they had licked Primus, jug and spoons till they were clean and gleaming, which they had not been for a long time.

There was little doubt that Girly was the prime mover in this base theft, for she knew where the provisions were kept and, no doubt, what the different boxes contained; for Girly was very clever and made good use of her eyes. As we entered the tent and saw the awful thing that had happened, Girly lay on her back, waving her paws in wheedling apology. Grimrian and Bjørn had taken up quarters in our sleeping bags, where they were sleeping the heavy sleep of repletion, snoring loudly and smelling abominably. Bitter was the awakening, for the whip handles were still relatively whole, though the long lashes had been eaten. That last did not matter so much at that moment, since it was only the whip handles we needed; as a means of punishment they exactly suited our state of mind. We were furious. Our arms were strong and the presumptious ones were duly taught that that particular crime could not go unpunished. In order that justice should be administered impartially, I thrashed Iver's Bjørn and he my Girly. Grimrian's punishment was left to the last, but he got what he deserved, first from Iver, then from me, so there was no question of his getting off lightly.

We could scarcely sleep for the stench in our sleeping bags and for vexation. The next morning there was no question of our being able to sledge on. Our thieving dogs were incapable of hauling properly, being still too gorged and, perhaps, also rather tender from the payment we had exacted; thus, whether we liked it or not, the dogs had to have a day's rest, lovely and fine though the weather was. I found it impossible to sit still, so leaving the tent, I set off in the hope of finding a relatively practicable way down the huge wall of ice that towered up vertically from the land below. The previous day's experience of leaving the dogs to guard our belongings had proved too expensive for us to dare leave them alone again, so Iver had to remain in camp to keep an eye on the tent, provisions and dogs. He would have liked to come with me, partly because of the joy of setting foot on true land again, but mostly so as to be there to help, if I happened to come unawares too close to a crevasse, as I very easily could. "I don't like your going alone," said Iver, "So much can happen. And what then?"

Yes, what then? If it happened, it happened, and that was all there was to it, for we dared not leave the dogs alone with the food.

I walked off across the glistening, steeply shelving ice, and after several hours I found a promising place, where a huge snowdrift had made a sort of bridge from the bottom of a winding gorge in the sheer wall of the ice to the land below. It looked probable that we could reach the land by going through the gorge and so on across the snow drift, but, however tempting, I did not dare try it, for it was so steep that I was afraid I would be unable to climb up on to the ice again and get back to Iversen.

It was hard to have to turn when the goal of our longings was so close, but, nonetheless, I was in high spirits as I made my way back to Iver, and I shouted to him from a distance: "Tomorrow we make our last start on this waste of ice — and before evening we'll camp on a carpet of heather." Promising words, almost too promising and arrogant to come true, but we had been through too hard a school not to rejoice, when we thought there was anything to rejoice at.

For a while, indeed, it looked as though I had spoken too soon, as though all my fine promises were written in the finest drift snow. The sun was shining, the dogs were rested and our excitement had somehow or other communicated itself to them, when with tails waving they started off at a run across the steeply shelving ice. The thrill of speed laid hold of my team; wilder and wilder grew the pace, while I pulled back against them as hard as I could, for I knew that the vertical glacier wall, 300 feet high, was close, and just exactly where we were heading at that crazy speed.

The sledge rolled and yawed like a boat in a storm. The ice was now all but bare of snow, worn by the drifting snows of winter and as smooth as a mirror. The dogs noticed nothing; they no longer obeyed, just ran on and on; perhaps they, too, had caught the smell of land. Then I slipped, fell and was dragged along, for I could not get free of the trace which, as always, I had over my shoulder. I was dragged along over the hard, smooth ice, banging myself here and everywhere, until at last the trace broke. That was a relief, for I knew that at least I was not going to be dragged down to certain death. I lay where I was to collect my wits after the wild chase and watched the sledge continue its mad career downhill, till suddenly the stem tilted into the air and vanished as abruptly as did the joyous barking of the dogs.

I was too battered and bruised to be able to get to my feet at once, but I realized that Iver must be halted, if that were in any way possible, so that his sledge should not be lost too. If it were, we would be lost as well. I got to my feet with a tremendous effort. I turned and twisted, bent low down and far back in an attempt to discover whether I really had escaped from my rough ride without any broken bones or other serious injury; I squeezed myself here and there on the body's most vulnerable spots, but it was obvious that I was not badly hurt in any way.

It was impossible to keep your feet on that mirror-smooth slope of ice, so I had to crawl on hands and knees, hooking on to the least protuberance in order to get up to the crest of the rise: then at last I saw Iver, thank goodness, without his sledge.

When he came up, he asked in a horrified voice: "What's happened to the sledge and the dogs?"

"Gone over the glacier face, smashed, dead. And I nearly went the same way," I replied, dully, rubbing my bruised body. "We've lost everything there was on my sledge. It's almost the worst thing that could have happened, and we've been rejoicing so at reaching land today!"

Iver would not believe that things were so bad. "Are you sure?" he asked, in a voice that was slightly shaky — "Don't you think they might have got away with the fall?" No, I did not. I had seen the rear end of the sledge tilt high in the air, as if it were a ship diving to the bottom. They did not have a chance, unless a miracle had happened. At that moment, Iver cried out joyfully and slid a few paces forward across the smooth ice. There really had been a miracle. Ten yards away lay the sledge, overturned on top of a dog that, unable to keep up the frantic pace, had got under a runner, and thus acted as a brake. The poor dog was whimpering pitiably, as it had every reason to do, for the sledge was heavy. And in front of the sledge sat my Girly with her tongue hanging far out from her flews, almost grinning as she looked at me, as much as to say "What a speed, wasn't it?"

It took us eight hours of really hard work with all the dogs harnessed to the one sledge to haul it up the ice slope, down which I had driven, slid, almost flown in just a few minutes. But the land was beckoning to us, and, the weather being still fine, we had to go on. Off we went on another reconnaissance, and after we had cut some 350 steps, each eighteen inches or so, in the glassy ice or hard, compressed snow, we reached the foot of the ice-wall and land that was free of snow and to us a paradise.

Willows grew in our paradise, a whole little copse of willows three or four hands high and with trunks as thick as a thumb that was swollen with frostbite and unnaturally thick. Long stalks of grass stuck up through the snow and their rime powdered seed-cases waved gently in a warm wind. On the bare patches, we saw thick layers of moss, naturally frozen hard, but as soon as the sun regained its warmth, they would melt and become soft, moist and summery and be an invitation to rest. Our eyes were gladdened by the sight of lovely tall heather in the particularly well-sheltered spots, not fifty yards from the eternal ice.

When we also found a well trodden hare's path, we uttered joyous cries that rang across that deadly silent land, and at the sight of fresh musk ox tracks and the smell of fresh, almost warm musk ox droppings, our joy knew no bounds. That there were also lots of tracks of the hares' and musk oxen's grim followers, the fox and the wolf, was only in the order of things. They, too, were greeted with delight, for so many tracks of beasts of prey were warranty for the presence there of many herbivorous creatures.

To our eyes, this was a fertile land immensely rich in animal life; yet just behind us stood the all but vertical face of the glacier, 1,000 feet high and exhaling the searing breath of the inland ice. The edge of the ice gleamed white and blue in the sunlight; it was beautiful to look at, yet the outpost of the dead and desolate inland ice, a place abandoned by the gods and soon to be abandoned by us as well.

It was not easy to leave so wonderful a spot, but we could not enjoy it to the full while our sledges were still up on the inland ice, so laboriously we clambered back to them. Whipping up the dogs, we drove down towards the gorge through which we had just come — and halted spellbound: the sun was standing right above a dip in the ice, and its rays were pouring in between the tall ice-cliffs straight towards us. There was a sparkling and glittering on the mirror-smooth, crystal-clear banks, the ice-crystals which, as numerous as the sands of the sea, caught the sun's rays and reflected them in condensed, blazing splendour. Wherever we looked was the flash and sparkle of light and colour; it was like a fantastically lavish firework display, something out of the Arabian Nights, like all the fireflies of the Tropics and all the phosphorescence of the seas.

So much beauty almost took our breath away, and we sat down on our sledges to enjoy the magnificent spectacle. Thus it was that the inland ice took leave of two exhausted travellers, to whom the journey across its immense mass had been like a month-long nightmare. This was showing us an entirely new face, a side of the ice we did not know at all, a brilliant bemusing sight that branded itself upon eye and mind and cannot be forgotten as a nightmare can.

And yet one should be able to forget it, for, after all, it was merely splendour stolen from the glorious sun and ought not to have impressed those who, in toil and pain, had made the acquaintance of the Ice King's accursed and merciless realm. But even though we knew it was a fraud, we could not do other than delight in the display; it was such a blaze that you almost felt it must set the ice on fire, at the least melt it. We enjoyed the spectacle, but the lure of the land was stronger still. The dogs were got up again, the whip lash slipped across their backs: "Forget it, dogs, it's only a damned lie. The inland ice is not like that."

So we slithered down through the gorge, the sledges creaking and groaning. Though the sun was still shining brightly, it seemed as though it were refusing to have anything more to do with the fraud, for when we came into an ice-glen which lay in a direction different than that in which the firework display was being given, every sparkling gleam of light was extinguished, and around us the ice was as naked ice is — cold, hard and glassy, evil and grim, a realm of death from which man should keep away.

We wriggled the sledges downwards along narrow, sinuous beds of streams eaten out of the smooth ice by the foaming torrents of summer. We toiled with those sledges, onward and downward, using their own weight to propel them, edging them between walls of ice where it was scarcely wide enough to take them, and though we gradually took off more and more of our things until we were half undressed, the sweat was pouring off our bodies. We struggled hard to get away from the accursed ice and down to the land so temptingly bare of ice and snow, with its beautiful vegetation and tracks of other live creatures. At length, after many hours' toil, we emerged from the winding gorge. The walls of ice opened out, as though the inland ice were giving up any further attempt to hold us back, and the long hard bridge of snow linking the hated ice with the land lay in front of us; could we let the sledges take this last hurdle in one glorious rush, or should we be careful and lower them down?

We looked at the steep fall, measured the distance to the ice-free land with our eyes, but we were fagged and wanted to have it over and done with, so we closed our minds to the voice of caution and common sense, let the sledges balance on the brink for a moment and then gave them a shove. Off we rushed down the snow drift in a smother of swirling snow, and with the wind whistling round our ears, we swept right out on to the land, to the willow bushes, to the waving stalks of grass with their heavy rime-encrusted seed-cases, to the heather on which we had been so greatly looking forward to pitching our tent, so that, for the first time for ages, we might lie on a bed of something other than ice.

It went all right, except that the dogs could not keep up with that breakneck speed and some of them were run down by their own sledge and got under the runners. They yelled a bit as the sledge, weighing five or six hundredweight, squeezed them into the hard snow. It must have hurt, but it also braked the sledge and that was badly needed. And, besides, such treatment has no great effect on sledge dogs. They can take the most incredible blows and bumps and squeezes, and ours had all suffered much worse things up there on the inland ice that none of us would ever tread again, if we could help it.

CHAPTER VIII

On Land Again

Fertile land — Musk oxen — Orgy — Snow-blindness —
Sledging over land — Harbingers of spring — Danmarks Fjord

How we revelled in it all; the heather, the grass and the dwarf willow copse that to us looked a wood, the sunshine and being able to walk safely where we liked without having to be everlastingly on the watch for bottomless chasms, and always being prepared to hear a warning shout of "Crevasse." The dogs enjoyed it all as much as we did. Now they were allowed to run around freely, for there was no danger there of their disappearing into some gaping crevasse from which there was no escape.

They made full use of their freedom, smelling the heather, the grass and the willows, cocking their legs as is the way of dogs, and giving full vent to their joy as they roamed around, uttering little joyful whimpers over the lovely things they were finding, sniffing at the tracks of hares and musk oxen and scampering back to us as though to tell us of the wonderful experiences and smells of that extraordinary day, which had begun in the grey of morning up on the eternal ice, 1,170 feet above where we were, and had ended in the glow of the evening sun on fertile land.

We pitched our tent, brought armfuls of heather to make a bed softer and more heavenly than any we had ever lain on, lit a little fire of fragrant heather, cooked some pemmican and ate, laughing and revelling in it all, then rolled over in our sleeping bags as we swallowed the last mouthful, and fell asleep from sheer joy and exhaustion. And it was no wonder that we were exhausted, for it had taken us thirty-six hours' uninterrupted struggling to get down off the inland ice.

So happy were we, that we soon woke again; and how we revelled in being there, despite our aching limbs! The sun was shining on to our little tent and it was warm inside it. A few midges were humming round us; perhaps they had come out a little too early, but it was a sort of spring, summer even for us, and a large bumble bee was already busy about whatever is its purpose in life.

We had been looking forward to reaching land as much as if we had been shipwrecked and in the utmost distress on a foaming, storm-whipped sea. Great as had been our expectation, it was as nothing compared with the delight of reality. And that is a thing that seldom happens to me.

There was, however, one little snake in our Garden of Eden. The firework display given by the inland ice, and the many hours we had spent out on snow and ice glittering with sunlight had been too much for my eyes; they had been prickly and sore when I went to sleep but, when I woke up, they were horribly painful, as though fine salt and pepper had been sprinkled on them.

How I cursed! Here was I wanting my eyes for revelling in the beauties of God's nature and well on the way to being snow-blind! I should have to be very careful. A bandage over my eyes would soon put them right and some drops of cocaine would relieve the pain. But, nevertheless, it was a sad business having to sit in the lovely sunshine outside the tent and not be able to see all the glories around me.

Iver helped me as well as he could, talking the whole time. "See here," he said to me, who could not see, "here's the loveliest heather. And here's such a big willow, and over there by the slope to the left is taller grass than any we've yet seen."

We had to have at least one quiet day so that my snow blindness might pass off, and also we had solemnly promised the dogs that they should have a whole day's rest when we reached land, and that promise had to be kept; thus it made little difference that my eyes also made it essential to stay where we were for a day; so we made a virtue of necessity, rested and enjoyed the delight of the dogs, the sun and the fact of having got down to land.

Suddenly, Iver exclaimed in a voice that trembled with excitement.

"Look, see there! Don't you see the cows?" "Cows?" I thought angrily and said so too, "Has the inland ice robbed you of your senses, Iver, or are you dreaming of your family's farm in Jutland?"

"No, no," cried Iver, "you must be able to see them. There they are again!" Iver was so excited that it was obvious there must be something, so cautiously I lifted the bandage from my eyes and just caught a glimpse of what, to my painful, watering eyes, looked like two large stones. Iver said they were cows, he meant musk oxen but, in his joy, had forgotten where we were. He thrust a rifle into my hand and, while I floundered along behind, he ran on ahead. A shot rang out, and so I too shot at the nearest stone, which seemed as big as a haystack and impossible to miss, even for someone who was half blind. Iver gave a joyful yell. He had been right; they were musk oxen and one was dead, the other wounded and soon dead as well. And then there was feasting in the land!

The dogs went quite wild at the sight and smell of blood and meat. They ate till their bellies were almost bursting, paused for a moment to recover, then ate again, digging into the carcase of the big bull till they had blood and shreds of meat sticking to their heads and bodies. They ate on and on until they collapsed, exhausted and gasping, then they slept for a while, snoring loudly, woke themselves with their snores and went on eating.

It was a magnificent feast. There was a heavenly smell in our tent, as Iver cooked us steaks an inch thick. As we ate them, the juice ran down our chins and over our fingers, which we licked clean. And then we ate some more, threw the bones out to the dogs which could scarcely bother to touch them. That feast of ours on the fringe of the inland ice was worthy of the heroes in Valhalla.

As dogs and men fell asleep in utter repletion, the news of the feast went out over the land to its wild creatures, the foxes and wolves. They came from afar to our little camp and carried on where we and the dogs had given up, feasting undisturbed. The dogs did not even resent the fact that their close but hated relatives had come unbidden to their feast. Thus, if one of them, waking from its sleep of repletion, felt an urge to eat and went on again, dog and fox would each be so occupied with eating, that neither paid any attention to the presence of the other.

We could not stay long, though, and once we had more or less recovered from our repletion, we harnessed the dogs to the sledges and drove off across the lake, to which chance had brought us. We took one last look at the inland ice, glad to be rid of the sight of it, however lovely it now was in the bright sunshine.

We now saw nothing but high and lovely land on either shore of the lake, rounded hillocks covered with grass and heather; every step revealed something new and pretty to go into ecstasies over — it was, indeed, different from the dead and desolate expanse of the inland ice.

And see! There on the slope was a herd of musk oxen grazing within range, big stolid bulls, sure-footed cows and slight heifers and some small, new-born calves as well. We sat down on the slopes to enjoy the sight of the splendid creatures. They seemed to be playing, though it looked a dangerous game; and there were a couple of bulls who were especially fierce.

They backed away from each other, sharpened their horns on large stones and then thundered across the ground straight at each other and collided head on. The impact was so violent that both bulls were forced almost vertically up on their hind legs. The noise of it aroused echoes far and wide, yet long before the last of them had died away in a whispering, the two bulls had forgotten they were fighting and had taken to grazing, though glaring balefully at each other as they cropped the grass. They could not eat long, however, but had to have another trial of strength; they were the males fighting for the favour of the females.

It was tempting for us to intervene, but the sledges were already piled with meat and we hoped that, if we shewed moderation that day, luck would smile on us when we had real need for game.

We had been so hungry ourselves that we did not want to kill unless absolutely necessary, and so we decided to let the musk oxen live. We put our hands to our mouths and uttered great bellows that echoed from mountain to mountain. The musk oxen paused in their trial of strength and looked wonderingly at the strange noisy creatures who had burst in upon their domain. They did not feel altogether happy in our vicinity, yet they walked along the hillside quite quietly, snatching mouthfuls as they went and so disappeared over the crest.

We were pleased and proud of our self-control, and hoped most heartily that, in some days' time, when we should be without meat again, it would be rewarded.

We sledged on northwards towards Danmarks Fjord, following a long, narrow lake, little more than a broad river bed, surrounded by a confusion of domed hilltops with little valleys in between. Near us, all round us, we saw signs of spring's arrival, saw it in the delicate greenish garb that the domed hilltops and valleys were on the point of assuming. The grass and the heather were beginning to sprout, and the willows, the lovely little willows, were covered with catkins. We heard the coming of spring in the slight drip and trickle of water in every furrow upon the rounded hilltops, where moss and lichen were green on the sunny side, but still frozen and grey where they faced the mountain and the icy north. And some small birds were chirruping joyfully in the golden sunshine that filled the valley and caressed the blunt tops of the hills.

We rejoiced in the spring and when, every hour or so, we halted for a short rest, we sat and revelled in the sight of that lovely land and of the huge masses of mountains far to the east and west standing up blue and cold against the light shimmering spring sky; meanwhile the dogs bustled about to the extent of their traces, till they found a nice spot smelling of spring on which to lie. The harsh inland ice was already forgotten by both men and dogs.

Every now and again we clambered up an eminence to see what awaited us beyond, where the lake disappeared behind a large black mountain-side — often we caught a glimpse of Danmarks Fjord, the high Sjællands Mountains and the black nose of Cape Holbaek bathed in a strip of bright sunshine, a magnificent sight. As we lay there in the heather enjoying the rest, the spring, the sunshine and the view of the nearby mountains and the others in the distance, my thoughts went back to that other autumn when Mylius-Erichsen, Høeg-Hagen and

Brønlund had been making their way from the north towards the very parts where we now were, looking for the inland ice which we had just left so gladly, but which they had thought was the road to deliverance, the shortest way to a snug ship and their comrades.

What had their thoughts been on those dark, cold and stormy days, when they were where we now lay sunning ourselves? Were they prepared for the fate that awaited them up there on the merciless inland ice? Had they lost hope of being able to get through, or were they still animated by the optimism which is so general among polar travellers, who always believe that, somehow or other, they will manage, however dark and uncertain the outlook may be at the time.

And how had they got up on to the inland ice in the autumn, when the sunshine and floods of summer must have melted the great snow-drifts like that we had successfully come down? And where was the long, dead glacier which Brønlund mentioned in his journal, the place which, when they saw it in the distance, they had thought would provide easy access up on to the inland ice?

We had not seen it. On the contrary, the place where we now were, and where they had been three years before, was bounded to the south by an almost vertical wall of ice, at least a thousand feet high, and no ascent of it was possible, not even where we had come down. Had the dead, flat glacier for which they had been making been an optical illusion? Had refracted light conjured up the vision of a practicable route where no way existed?

It was pointless to puzzle one's head over this but, nevertheless, my thoughts kept turning to the three unfortunate men, who had been as young and as fond of life as we. They had succumbed to the cold somewhere between the place where we now stood and the sheer, black mountains at Lamberts Land, on the same route as that along which we had just come. We, however, had travelled at a time of relatively good weather and with good equipment; yet the inland ice had given us toil and trouble enough. Mylius and his companions were going in the opposite direction, and that at a time of darkness, cold and storm, with wretched clothing, no nourishing food, no dogs. They probably still had hope that they would get through somehow or other, but they couldn't have had much faith in their doing so.

A cloud drifted across the heavens, slid across the sun and the land became dark and drear and cold. Resting was no longer pleasant and, as we walked down the mountain-side back to the lake and our sledges, we found little to say. What lay ahead of us might also prove difficult to come through.

We sledged on. The barking of the dogs awakened the echoes among the mountains, and the act of working drove all vain and morbid thoughts from our heads.

The going was hard but possible. We had had difficult sledging before and would have it again, before we got across the mountain ahead of us, the last before Danmarks Fjord. To this we came in time, struggled up its steep slopes on which there was little snow, and at last reached the crest and looked out across the vast expanse of ice encompassed by tall, grim mountains, which was Danmarks Fjord and our goal.

Then the sledges swept with a rush down a snowdrift, shot across a tide-water fissure and, before we realized what was happening, we had left the land and were back once more on sea ice!

CHAPTER IX

In Danmarks Fjord

*No game — We find the first cairn — Speculation on the dead
men's behaviour — We find the second cairn — Where Mylius-Erichsen spent
the summer — The fate of their diaries*

While we were still on the inland ice, we had envisaged sledging in
Danmarks Fjord as a sort of ideal journey in a paradise of security,
where meat was to be had whenever necessary. The reality did not
quite come up to those joyful expectations, but then, any paradise to
which you look forward in the hour of trial usually proves far less
lovely than you had imagined.

On the sea ice of Danmarks Fjord we were, of course, relieved of
any fear of crevasses, and for that we were duly grateful. The cold,
too, was less and the storms far from as violent as on the inland ice,
but otherwise there was no great difference between existence up there
half way to heaven and that where we now struggled over the sea ice
parallel with the land, where we expected and hoped to find traces of
our three predecessors.

Fear of what would happen to us, two lone men, had followed us
across the inland ice as one of two very depressing, invisible companions whom we found it impossible to shake off. We had hoped,
however, to leave them behind up there, but such fear is not so easily
shaken off; even down on the sea ice, where we felt safe from crevasses
and many other horrors which only the inland ice could produce, we
found that our invisible shadow was still with us, whispering ominous
warnings about everything we did.

It was a different fear that accompanied us now, not fear of crevasses
but fear that our labours would be in vain, that that which we had
struggled to find, hoped to find, been sure of finding, was nonetheless

not to be found. Were that to be the case, it would be hard to bear, even though the fault could not be ours.

Once fear has entered into you, it easily becomes hydra-headed, and each head speaks only words of ill omen. One voice was busy whispering to us what we knew very well but kept trying to put from us, that the dogs would be unable to carry on much longer, and that we still had a good seven hundred miles to Shannon Island. Another voice kept muttering that, of course, we would not come across the game we had to have to get through. Not even Mylius and his companions had got enough to save their lives, and one of them was a Greenlander and knew far more about Greenland hunting than either of us. Without game, our sledges would soon be bare of food either for men or dogs. And the warning voice muttered something about imagining what our feelings would be on the day when we had used up all our cartridges without hitting anything, so that we were left without even the possibility of getting more food, about starvation and the consequences of that — which, of course was obvious, because we would still be nearly seven hundred miles from Shannon, the only place on that coast where we knew for certain that food was to be had.

When we looked at each other's somewhat ravaged faces, there came another voice with a horrible question: Have you, foolhardy man, thought what it would mean if your companion got lost in the mist, when he was out hunting alone? Or if he broke a leg in the pack ice? Or suppose he fell ill? What would you do? Would you leave him where he was, or would you try to get him to Shannon? And what would he do, if you fell ill? *Are* you not ill already? What, otherwise, are those queer pains you have? Why else do you feel so unutterably tired? That's no natural tiredness! And remember, you are more than seven hundred miles from the ship at Shannon! Do you really think that one of you could get a sick companion there, if an accident should happen?

Fools, if you think that! But you are great fools, so remember that your dogs will die soon. And you cannot possibly think that you can save a sick companion after that. Better give it up straight away.

And how would you like being left alone up here in this incredibly vast wilderness? Just imagine how awful that must be. Do you remember that day on the inland ice when you did not know where Iver was? And how you felt then? He was only gone for a short time, scarcely an hour, but long enough for you to be able to imagine what it would be like to have to stumble on alone all the seven hundred miles to Shannon Island.

That was an appalling thought, and each time we were left alone, even for a short while, fear whispered to us: Imagine what it will be like if he does not come back. You will be alone like the dead in their graves — and yet above. It will be awful.

At other times, another voice muttered something about our skins and sleeping bags, which had been whole and good when we left the ship, now being so torn and worn that the wind whistled through great holes in the skins and the sleeping bags kept shedding handfuls of hair. They were, perhaps, still good enough for summer use, the voice said, but seven hundred miles was a very, very long way to have to pull a sledge with only weak dogs, or no dogs at all. Progress would be very slow, if we could even force our sledge along. And perhaps we might have to spend a winter as well as a summer on the coast, and what then?

Then the many-tongued ghost had no need to say more, for we knew exactly how things would go then — hundreds of miles from Shannon Island.

The ghost found it easy to affect us in our weakened state with its ominous mutterings. Perhaps I was the easier prey, for I had the moral responsibility for Iver's relative welfare, and also I felt so strangely and inexplicably tired, so tired that I could scarcely get going in the mornings and felt tired all day long.

Such thoughts are not healthy for people sledging seven hundred miles from their base, and they have to be knocked on the head before they get too much of a hold. Work is a good medicine for morbid thoughts, so we threw our weight into the traces and toiled with the sledges and the tired dogs, shouting at them so as to put the silence to flight, labouring to cover a few miles of the many hundreds we had to cover before we could stop struggling.

That did not help so very much, for it just allowed another of our grim, terrible companions to make itself felt all the more — hunger. Always we could hear its urgent voice feel its pressure when our stomachs were empty, as they were almost all the time. The musk oxen meat, which had come like a gift from Heaven, when we escaped down off the inland ice, was long since eaten. And, for the time being, the gods were not being lavish with their gifts, even though some days before we had magnanimously given two musk oxen their lives, relying on being in the gods' good graces.

As we sledged along the coast, our eyes were fixed on the land we were passing, carefully scrutinizing everything we could not immediately identify. Nothing could escape our watchful gaze, whether it was edible or the thing we had come so far to find: traces of the missing men.

We saw no musk oxen either on the slopes of the mountains which rose fairly steeply from the line of the coast, nor in the places where the rim of mountains was broken to make way for a little flat ground. Nor did we see any of their tracks when together we walked deep into the land to where we had seen something we thought resembled a musk ox. Or could that be a cairn, perhaps, that tall pointed thing there, like a stone?

Many a time our searching eyes were fooled into thinking they saw one or the other, and every time we were disappointed: what we had thought was a musk ox, or what we took to be a cairn set up by the missing men, were nothing but large, moss-grown stones.

And there were innumerable stones, big stones, stones like musk oxen and stones like cairns — and just as many disappointments.

There was nothing but disappointment there in Danmarks Fjord, the place to which we had looked forward so much. The going was very heavy and our daily distances were all too small, inhuman though our labour was. Even the weather was a disappointment, for it was far rougher than it should have been at that time of year. Grey-black clouds hung low above our heads, the wind was quite stiff and almost continually in our faces; snow fell and drifted, not dry snow as fine as dust, as on the inland ice, but moist, clammy snow that caked on our clothes, in our beards and hair.

We toiled slowly along, wasting many hours investigating every stone that stood out in any way, for it might well have been a cairn. And when mist hid the land, we halted lest we should pass a cairn or other trace of the missing men, and also to give the dogs a badly needed rest.

In the end, our hard staring was rewarded. Some distance away, on a shoulder of the mountain, we saw what could not possibly have been a musk ox, but was possibly a cairn. When we eventually reached the spot, we flung down our traces and hurried up the steep slope to what we had so long had our eyes on and which we could now see was indeed a cairn.

Beside the cairn lay a large piece of drift-wood and several smaller bits of wood. Were we to be disappointed again? Had Mylius and his companions merely raised the cairn so that they could find the wood again, once the autumn snow had fallen? Or did it perhaps contain the communication from the missing men, which we were hoping and expecting to find in the fjord?

We could scarcely believe that we were so close to our objective. Carefully we loosened a couple of stones from the foot of the cairn, so that we could peer inside. To our delight, we saw a cartridge lying on a flat stone. That could only be a message from the men who had vanished in the wilderness of ice.

Carefully we opened the cartridge and picked out the tightly rolled piece of paper inside; then we sat down on a stone and read Mylius-Erichsen's confident message, written just before they had left that place. But let him tell it himself:

DANMARKS FJORD, CIRCA 81° 25 N.

SEPTEMBER 12, 1907

Today, Hagen, Brønlund and the undersigned, all fit and well, leave this place, called Wolf Hill, with one sledge and seven dogs, to start our journey back to the ship on new and, today at long last, safe ice. Since leaving our summer camp about eleven Danish miles [circa 51 miles] from here, on August 8, we have had to kill seven dogs for food to keep ourselves and

the surviving dogs going, while lying out on the sea ice, half
a mile from land, where we were halted for 16 days by water
on the ice. Finally, on August 25, we reached land and shot
four hares. Since then, we have moved camp in short marches,
totalling some thirty-five miles, up Danmarks Fjord, continually hindered in our progress towards more favourable hunting
grounds by mild weather and impassable new ice and latterly
by open water from coast to coast. We have been on foot across
the mountains, followed by the dogs, for a further forty-five
miles up the fjord to Sjællands plain, shooting in all 15 young
ptarmigan, 15 hares, 1 wolf and 8 musk oxen (2 bulls, 3 cows
and 3 calves); we camped a week in the open, cooking with
drift-wood, which we found in abundance along the shore,
fed the dogs up and brought meat and suet to this place, which
is the most southerly point in the fjord we have been able to
reach by sledge. The ice further in is still unsafe, but we had
thought of possibly returning via the inland ice from the head
of Danmarks Fjord to the fjord on 79° N. Presume we have
had up to 15° below (Celsius) in the last few weeks. Are carrying on the sledge drift-wood for eight days' cooking and over
300 lbs. of meat, sufficient to feed us for 16 days and the dogs
for 8 days. Are following the bay east to the outer coast, some
170 miles, and with the depots we laid there in the spring and
what bear we can shoot, hope to be able to reach the ship safe
and sound in 5 or 6 weeks.

L. MYLIUS-ERICHSEN,
Leader of "*Danmark* Expedition"

Conditions had obviously been reasonably good for the three men
there, and they had found quite a lot of game. They had left the little
headland where we now were, hoping, with considerable justification,
that they would be able to win through and return to their ship safe
and sound.

The three had left the headland on September 12, heading up Danmarks Fjord, looking for a way out. We had two other dates to help trace their progress till death overtook them. One of them was given in Jørgen Brønlund's diary, which ended by recording that the three men —

On October 19, in the afternoon, arrived up on the inland ice; the ascent took four days. The fifth of our remaining dogs is now dead, gored by a musk ox. The sun no longer gets above the horizon.

The next and last date (November 15) shows that the journey across the inland ice, from where they climbed up from Danmarks Fjord to the sea ice just north of Lamberts Land, took at the most 26 days, for Jørgen Brønlund wrote just before he died:

Succumbed at 79 Fjord after attempting return across inland ice in November. I arrived here in fading moonlight and could go no further because of frost-bitten feet and the dark. The bodies of the others are to be found in front of the glacier in the middle of the fjord (about 12 miles). Hagen died November 15 and Mylius some 10 days after.

Mylius-Erichsen and his two companions had thus been sledging in Danmarks Fjord from September 12 to October 19, thirty-seven days in all. According to the message we found in the cairn at Wolf Hill, the three men left there with seven dogs quite confident of being able to sledge northwards out of Danmarks Fjord. They intended to take with them enough meat for sixteen days' personal use and eight days' feed for the dogs, as well as drift-wood to last for the same period. That was not much, yet enough for them to have been able to reach their most northerly depot on the outer coast (at the north-east rounding) some 160 miles from Wolf Hill. That, of course, is a considerable distance to

sledge when you have provisions for only sixteen days and your strength
and endurance have been diminished by the hardships of summer. The
latter could possibly, even probably, be offset somewhat by the fact that
sledging conditions are normally relatively good in the early autumn.
The new ice usually provided good going at the end of September,
when, too, the weather was normally good and the days relatively long.
These factors should all have helped them to get to their most northerly
depot, which they never did reach, for we later found it untouched.

On the other hand, autumn sledging across relatively freshly frozen
ice always entails, especially along the unprotected outer coast, a certain
risk that storm or heavy swell will destroy the new ice and its good
sledging conditions, with the result that a sledge party can be forced to
halt for several days till the ice becomes practicable again. It may well
have been this that forced the three men to change their plans and give
up the attempt to reach the depot on the north-east rounding, the route
that presumably would have saved them, since they had a string of well-
supplied caches to carry them on. We know, however, from Brønlund's
journal that, instead of going all out to reach the cache that would have
saved them, the three men made their way back to the inner arm of
Danmarks Fjord, in order to get up on to the inland ice.

It can hardly have been acute shortage of provisions that made the
three change their plan and their route, for they left Wolf Hill in
Danmarks Fjord with seven dogs and we know from the next, and last,
entry in Brønlund's journal that they still had five dogs when they were
climbing up on to the inland ice, for he wrote "the fifth of our remaining dogs is now also dead, gored to death by a musk ox."

Thus, in thirty-seven days, the number of their dogs had been
reduced by only two, which must mean that hunting had been good
enough to have provided meat to feed the dogs for about a month and
enough for themselves for at least a fortnight. Unless they had that
much, they would certainly have killed the dogs to feed themselves and
the remaining dogs; yet, from September 12 when they left Wolf Hill,
to the second last entry in Jørgen Brønlund's journal (October 19), their
team had been reduced by only two.

It is useless to speculate what were the causes of Mylius-Erichsen's and his companions' repeated alterations of plan and route, but they must obviously have had an awful time of it, if they came to see that there was less and less hope of their ever getting through, that they were just wasting the days in idle roaming across unknown land. More than a month passed before they finally seized the last desperate chance to break out of the magic circle in which they had been so long without finding a practical road to deliverance. Wherever they searched, they had found their road barred by high mountains, the inland ice or open water, and then, in a final attempt to escape, they had hauled themselves up on to the inland ice in November and headed through darkness, cold, storm and blinding snow — knowing full well that death followed in their tracks and must catch them up. As things had turned out, they were unable to wait for conditions to improve and let them get back to the ship via the coast. Iver was right when, after reading the message from the cairn, he exclaimed "Poor devils, so glad, so confident when they were here. And then what! What must they have suffered before the end came?"

There was nothing more to be found at the cairn, no reason to linger there, so we went back to our dogs. We had to press on. The find at the cairn meant that our search for traces of the missing men had not been in vain, but when we got back to the sledges, we were made painfully aware that we were likely to have our own problems to contend with before we got back to the ship, for we found one of the dogs dead of overwork.

That left us with only seven dogs and none of them good.

After four days of hard sledging, which cost the life of yet another dog, we finally reached a place which, as far as we could judge from Jørgen Brønlund's journal, was where the three had spent some agonizing summer months with hunger, uncertainty and doubt as their constant companions.

It was a desolate, gloomy place. There was not even the smallest willow to be seen, not a blade of grass, no vegetation of any kind but a little moss on the sunny side of the beds of the many streams that had dug themselves deep into the ground. Everywhere we found traces of a protracted stay: footmarks trodden deep in dry soil, cairns on every hill crest, small ends of rope, here and there a bone and a few scraps of material, both tent canvas and cloth. It was obvious that that had been a hunger camp, for each piece of cloth or rope, every bit of anything that could be swallowed had been gulped down by the omnivorous sledge dogs and had passed through them. If such food had not nourished, it had at least given the illusion of a full stomach for a short while.

We also found the three men's hearth: the iron tyre of a sledge-runner had been stuck in a can filled with stones and the end bent over so as to form a hook on which the cooking pot could hang. The actual hearth consisted of just two or three stones, between which there was still some ash and charred bits of wood and bone. They had burned everything that would burn.

Round the hearth were placed three dog-food boxes, empty of food but filled with stones. They made slightly better seats for the three to sit on at their fire than the local sharp-edged stones. A ring of stones near the hearth shewed where the tent had stood in 1907.

That was all. Seldom have I seen any place so desolate and depressing. In front of us lay the wide fjord, still an unbroken sheet of ice, but it was dull ice that was saturated with water and thus no pleasant sight for us who, in a few days' time, would have to chance our luck and try to cross it to some flat islands on the other side. That was not a cheerful prospect.

To the south stretched a monotonously flat coast with a stony fore-shore; to the north, the eye followed a somewhat higher, but equally uniform, coast to Cape Rigsdagen, a god-forsaken and unutterably gloomy place, far beyond which lay the most easterly part of Peary Land, just visible above the horizon.

All around us were a number of cairns, but the first, second and third that we opened were empty and so were the fourth and fifth — and we began to grow anxious. The place was incontestably the dead men's summer camp. They had stayed there for at least a couple of months, and it was there that we had expected to find a detailed report, perhaps also journals, for this was a likely place for them to have been left, as they would have been relatively easy to find, if the three failed to reach home.

There were plenty of cairns, but where could the report have been hidden?

Then we opened the last cairn which stood quite far inland, and there at last we found what we sought, what we had sledged so far to find: a thermometer case, well plugged, and in it an account of their energetic attempts to map as much as possible of the vast, unknown land — and of their heroic fight to maintain life during the couple of months that an evil fate and the arrival of summer had forced them to spend at that desolate and dismal spot.

That report should decide matters for us. Would it, we wondered, contain information that would compel us to continue on, or would it tell us that we had come to our journey's end and that we could now turn and try to make our way back, knowing that we had done everything we could be expected to have done.

This was what we read:

> On May 28, 1907, at the north-east promontory of this land (circa 82° 04 N. and 22 W.), Lieutenant Hagen, the Greenlander Brønlund and the undersigned parted company with Lieutenant Koch's sledge team, which had reached the northern point of Greenland and was on the way back to the ship at Cape Bismarck. We sledged westwards with 23 dogs until June 1 and reached Peary's Cape Glacier and discovered that Peary Channel does not exist, Navy Cliff is joined by land to Heilprin Land. We rechristened Independence Bay "Independence Fjord" and built a cairn (with a report) on a low headland near Cape Glacier. On the way out of the fjord, we discovered and explored two subsidiary fjords: Brønlund's Fjord to the north-west and Hagen's Fjord to the south-east, and built a cairn (containing a report) at the latter. Discovered old Eskimo tent rings.
>
> The sudden arrival of milder weather with deep snow and water on the ice, lack of game, illness and weakness among the dogs, hampered and delayed our journey out of the fjord,

with the result that we only reached this place on June 12. All further progress across the ice was by then impossible. Only 15 of the dogs were then still alive and another has died since. Since then, we have fed ourselves exclusively on game (7 musk oxen, 1 calf, 15 wild geese, 4 hares and 3 ptarmigan). Have done further surveying and added to our scientific collections with plants and fossils of plants and animals. Called the land "Crown Prince Christian's Land."

Not having got any large game since July 16, and being without further food for ourselves and the dogs, we must today leave this area, which is quite empty of game and which we have scoured for 25 miles around, and try to make our way to coastal areas with game — having first ferried ourselves on an ice-floe across to the continuous ice with our 14 dogs, 2 sledges and all our gear. We are all three perfectly fit and well. We shall try to get somewhat farther to the south-west up Danmarks Fjord, where we found plenty of hares and musk oxen to shoot, when we travelled it in May. If we can manage to get a sufficient supply of meat, we intend, when the ice finally becomes serviceable towards the end of the current month, to sledge the 580 miles or so back to the ship, which we hope to reach before the end of September, with or without dogs.

The cairns built here in the vicinity have been put up by Hagen for the purpose of trigonometric measurements and contain no reports.

We will leave accounts of our further fate in one or more cairns further up the fjord.

AUGUST 8, 1907. L. MYLIUS-ERICHSEN,
Leader of "*Danmark* Expedition to the North-east
Coast of Greenland, 1906–1908."

This statement, together with the information contained in the diary we had found on Brønlund's body at Lamberts Land, gave a fairly

Members of the *Alabama* expedition. From left, First Lieutenant Christian Jørgensen, Unger, Olsen, Aagarrd, Ejnar Mikkelsen, Poulsen, and Lieutenant Vilhelm Laub. Taken at Thorshavn, in the Faroe Islands.

Alabama in winter harbour at Shannon Island, 1910.

Sledding on new ice in the fall.

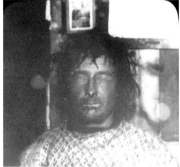

Mikkelsen and Iversen after the fall trip to Lambert's Land.

Laub's dog team and sled on the ice cap, April 7, 1910.

Paulsen and Olsen on the ice cap, April 9, 1910.

Mikkelsen and Iversen on the ice cap, April 9, 1910.

Girly   Grimrian

The cairn on the east coast of Danmark's Fjord, where the account of Mylius-Erichsen and his companions and their last activities was found.

Danmarks Fjord

Mt Mallemuk

The wreck of the *Alabama*.

The hut made from the *Alabama*'s wreck at Shannon Island.

complete picture of the three men's journeyings and work in the country round Danmarks Fjord, and of their intended return journey to their winter harbour, which had ended in their succumbing to hunger and cold in the dark days of November at Lamberts Land.

We could now turn and go back with an easy mind, for in Danmarks Fjord, in the whole of that huge area that lay spread before us, there was nothing more to find.

The men had taken their journals with them when they left the place where we now were, and they had taken them with them when they left Wolf Hill farther to the south, so they were certain to have taken them across the inland ice to their last camping place on the sea ice in front of the glacier at Lamberts Land. When Jørgen Brønlund left the camp there and his two dead companions, he took his own journal and the sketch maps they had made, which were common property. And so he had walked on alone through the darkness and cold — till he succumbed by the cache at Lamberts Land.

When, three years later, we reached the place where the camp must have been, we were too late. The thaws of three summers had melted the ice, or broken it up so that it had drifted out to sea with all that it carried.

All the anxious thoughts that had tormented the three men during the many dreary days of summer in Danmarks Fjord were reflected in Mylius-Erichsen's concise accounts, which he had written on his own behalf and that of his companions and deposited in a couple of cairns on the shores of that desolate land, hoping that they might be found if they themselves did not get through.

They were found, and when Iver and I stood with them in our hands, we were filled with the deepest admiration for the three who had fought so hard to explore unknown land, had conquered and paid for victory with months of wondering whether they would ever be able to get through to the cache that would save them, and fearing that their lives might be sacrificed in vain.

There was nothing more to be found in Danmarks Fjord, nothing more for us to do; we could now turn and try to get back to the ship seven hundred miles away in the south — and that, roughly, at the

same time of year as when the three dead men had tried to perform
the same journey.

We pitched our tent near the heart of the dead men's summer camp
and, as we lay in our sleeping bags, Iver and I spoke of their hopes,
disappointments and sufferings. But we were too tired and fagged to
be able to think of much beyond how we should fare on our journey
across the dull white surface, glistening with moisture, that had halted
and killed the three who had attempted it before us.

As we lay there in our sleeping bags, I again took up a matter that
had latterly occupied us greatly, and, for the last time, asked Iver what
he thought: should we go westwards in the hope of being able to reach
the Eskimos at Thule, or should we try to do what the dead men had
not been able to do — to make our way southwards along the coast to
our ship seven hundred miles away. The two routes were roughly of the
same length and, having explained all that was to be said in favour of
the one or the other, and the objections to either, I said something to the
effect that we should think well, for a mistake could cost us our lives.

Iver sat up in his sleeping bag, rubbed his eyes as if he had been asleep
during my long exposé of the pros and cons — as perhaps he had —
and said "You are skipper in this ship. Go east, if you think that best;
or west, if you like. I'll follow wherever you go, and I promise that, if
things go wrong, you'll never hear me say that perhaps it would have
been better if we had gone the other way."

The next day we started out on our homeward journey — heading
east.

CHAPTER X

Sledging in Slush

Scurvy and its consequences — Dogs and sledge in slush — Caches on the coast — Bear hunting — Early summer — Mt Mallemuk and deliverance

We had begun our return journey about June 1, leaving dreary Cape Rigsdagen in the west, and struggling across the mouth of Danmarks Fjord to the spot where our tent now stood on an island off flat ice-bound Crown Prince Christian's Land, a little black speck in the vast expanse of white that extended all around. Our dogs had found some dry spots, where they were resting after an arduous stage, during which they had hauled the sledges thirty miles through an appalling slush of deep watery snow. Iver was away hunting, hoping to get some meat for us and the dogs, who badly needed food with some nourishment in it, and meanwhile I was sitting on a rolled-up sleeping bag inside the tent, fighting dark thoughts about the future, which appeared so uncertain and gloomy.

Not uncertain, though, for as I sat there in our camp on that little island, seven hundred miles from our ship, there was little uncertainty about our future as far as I was concerned. I had discovered that I had been stricken by what is well-nigh the heaviest blow that can fall upon anyone sledging far from any place where help is to be had. I was ill, suffering from that bugbear of the early polar explorers and many a good man's death — scurvy.

For some time, I had had a fairly well-founded idea that all was not well with me, that the weariness that had come over me toward the end of the journey across the inland ice, and especially while sledging down Danmarks Fjord, was more than the natural consequence of the hard labour it had cost to get our sledges so far. Nor was it like me to anticipate misfortune, which was what I had done so often in Danmarks

Fjord, and that had made me wonder. Yet I had never for a moment suspected that illness might be the cause of my weariness and my gloomy view of the future, that I could have contracted scurvy.

But scurvy was what I had, and fairly badly at that: the tender, swollen joints, the vivid patches on legs and thighs, loose teeth and tender, bleeding gums, the giddiness when I hauled hard on the sledge, this all spoke a gloomy message there was no misunderstanding. I now sat on my sleeping bag, trying to remember what the medical handbook had had to say about the disease. But why did I bother? I did not have any of the things the handbook would tell me were necessary to cure the dread disease, nor any means of acquiring them. The only result of racking my brains was that I suddenly remembered that the description of the disease had contained, printed in italics, *"If immediate treatment is not given, scurvy will bring on fainting and end in death."*

So that was that, and there we were without medicine of any kind or any possibility of treatment or rest, and some seven hundred miles from the ship. But even if we had been at the ship, we would have had no effective medicines for scurvy, for people thought that modern tinned foods had put an end to that, and they were no longer carried. Yet if we were to get through to the ship, we should have to labour hard, far harder than a doomed man could manage. And what about Iver? He could hardly make his way back to the ship alone. In fact, there was no "hardly"; it was impossible for him to get through alone, so he too must die, if I died. And, in all probability, I was going to die of scurvy, as so many had before me. But, till then, I would be an intolerable burden round his neck. I would delay him, hold him back, drag him, my faithful companion, slowly but surely to destruction.

My head buzzed with such thoughts, and I sank deeper and deeper into the vortex of despondency; and when Iver returned empty-handed, I told him baldly what was wrong with me and what it meant to him.

He did not say much, though he must have thought a lot. The rapid dwindling of my strength had surprised him too, and he had long feared that it was illness and not just the toil that made me feel so tired and fagged. But he had never thought of it being scurvy either.

If there had been three of us, as had been the intention until Jørgensen got his feet so badly frost-bitten that he was crippled, the outlook would not have been quite so dark. Two men would naturally have had a far better chance of getting the sledge through to Shannon Island, even if I were lying on it, a mere extra burden. But one man alone? Impossible, quite impossible. He could never get there.

Again and again the thought returned, that perhaps I ought to have given up the journey to Danmarks Fjord when circumstances had changed and I found myself with only one man to accompany me — even though he was better than the best. But who can listen to the cautious voice of dull common sense, when you have already embarked on a venture that many considered impracticable? Not I, at least. Impracticable? Then it must be done. But luck had deserted us — and there was nothing more to be said.

It was two very silent men who crawled into their sleeping bags that night and found sleep long in coming. Iver was all that I had expected, and more. "Listen," he said, when he had got used to the idea, "it's bad, of course, with this damned scurvy. But I promise you that I shall do everything to help you, whatever happens to me. It is possible, too, that before very long we shall find game enough, and then you think that you would have a chance of recovery, don't you?"

He kept his word all through the subsequent long and critical month.

For the first few days, I still imagined that I could be of some help in hauling or pushing the sledge through the slush of snow; but it was not long before I had to recognize that as an illusion, and all that I could do then was to stumble on in front, in the hope of being able to trample a bit of a track for the dogs, perhaps even of discovering a better way, anything as long as I was not a burden.

However, I could not walk far in that dreadful going, and it was not long before I found myself unable to keep upright without the support of the sledge. Often I fell in the slush and was unable to get to my feet by myself, so that I lay in the icy mush until Iver came up and was able to help me to my feet. It was dreadful wanting to walk and not having the strength to do so.

A week later I had to give up attempting to manage by myself. I could no longer keep on my feet and was compelled to increase Iver's and the dogs' labour by adding my weight to what they were already scarcely able to drag through the dreadful slush of brash, snow and water, which persisted throughout June. However, I could still wield the whip as I sat on the sledge's load, and use my tongue to get the dogs to pull their best. But soon even that became too much for me, and when one day I fainted, I had no choice but to lie down on the sledge and let Iver put a rope round me and lash me on top of the load like a bundle, to prevent my falling off when the sledge rocked and swayed in the bottomless slush.

That was a blow and, as a veteran sledger who knew more than a thing or two, I ought to have felt ashamed, but I was so ill that I scarcely noticed what Iver did for me, how he shoved an anorak in under my head, when the sledge was bumping on rough ice, or how he wasted time and effort in finding the easiest going so that I should not suffer too much.

The dogs also had a hard time of it, and their strength dwindled with every day that passed. Slush and hunger can take the stuffing out of even the strongest dog, and it was long since any of ours had been strong.

The dreadful slush with which we had to contend all through June was also the poor dogs' greatest torment. Whenever the sledge stuck, as happened quite often, they crawled up on to it so as to get away from the intolerable, icy slush, and then they shook themselves, as is the way of dogs, and huddled close to me, soaking me, if I was not soaked already. This I usually was, for now and again I had to get off the sledge in order to lighten it when it was hopelessly stuck. Then I would sit on an ice-hummock or lie on the driest bit of ice to be found, while Iver stood up to his waist in the slush and struggled with the sledge; sometimes digging it out, baling slush out of the hole in which the sledge was stuck, or else trying to beat or tramp the stuff down so that it would bear the weight of sledge and dogs for the short moment necessary to get it out of the hole, calling and shouting to the dogs to pull and go on pulling.

Then, having got the sledge out of the hole in which it had stuck and halted it at a place where it did not sink in too deep, Iver would come back for me, always gay and cheerful, despite the labour and the water that poured off him. He would help me on to my feet and support me as, together, we stumbled to the sledge, on which I dropped heavily and let myself be lashed to it once again. So, by degrees, we moved on once more to the accompaniment of howls and cries, and the labour of it was so great that Iver fell silent to save his strength, and the dogs gasped with the effort.

Day after day, we sledged down the coast, a dreary coast without character, a low, flat glacier stretching for mile upon mile. The weather, too, was dark and dirty. Often there was snow, either large, wet flakes or fiercely driving drift snow, brought with the wind which came hooting off the glacier in a tardy unwelcome greeting from the bitterly cold interior. Nor were we spared mist and drizzle. Thus, for a month, we had slush under us, dampness around us, and dark clouds full of snow or rain hanging low above us; moisture and water above and below, moisture and water everywhere.

Luckily, we still had some provisions left — pemmican and a little tea, a few handfuls of biscuits, and that was our only comfort during those long laborious days. All day we longed for the moment when the pemmican could be served, unfortunately only half cooked in order to save precious fuel, but delicious even so. Our hunger was great and growing greater with every day, while our daily ration that had been small enough in the days of abundance, when the sledge was laden with food, had been more than halved when we began the return journey.

I longed for food but ate little, for the fat pemmican nauseated me and I could scarcely swallow a mouthful. I offered my ration to Iver, but he would not touch it. "We'll save that," he said, "till you recover and have to be fed up again."

Well, perhaps there might be something in that, but there did not seem much prospect of my ever getting fit again or requiring to be fed up. I was then losing consciousness more and more frequently.

Meanwhile, Iver struggled on down the coast, straining every muscle to get the sledge along, and every sense so as not to miss seeing the least hint of game or sign of the most northerly of the caches the *Danmark* Expedition had made for the use of Mylius-Erichsen and his companions on their return journey.

His efforts brought results in the shape of geese to put in the pot, and then, at last, the cache, the size of which came as an unpleasant surprise and made us fear for the future. Two pounds of pemmican, the same of kail and forcemeat and a pound of salami was all the cache contained. It was quite incomprehensible. I told Iver to have another look, that there must be more food in a cache made for famished sledgers. What we had found would have been little more than a snack for Mylius and his two companions, just enough to exacerbate their hunger. But there was no more, and we wondered and became more depressed than ever, for though we had not been able to find out before we left Copenhagen what these caches were supposed to contain, we had reckoned that there would be proper provisions at the places marked DEPOT on the official map of the *Danmark* Expedition.

The string of places thus marked had looked so reassuring on the map, even though the man who had made the most northerly of them had warned me that we would not be able to find them, and, for that reason, had refused to tell me what was in them. Even so, we had hoped that they would contain provisions if we ever found them, as we did. The contents of the two most northerly ones were ominously small.

Luckily, our disappointment was partially offset by two geese which Iver shot near the cache. But they did not last long. Our provisions were dwindling rapidly, and our dog food was almost all gone. There were a lot of geese where we were, and Iver would no doubt have been able to shoot more, if we had dared stay there for a couple of days — but we did not. We had to continue on our way without loss of time, southwards along the coast to Lamberts Land, which I hoped to be able to reach before it was too late. From there Iver might possibly make his way back to the ship alone, provided his nerve held.

So Iver struggled on down the coast, forcing the reluctant dogs through the slush of water and snow, pressing the sledge along while I lay lashed to it, a helpless dead weight that could neither fall off when the sledge was about to capsize in the slush, nor throw myself off when the fever was upon me.

Despite all his toil and exertions, Iver had always time to shove something soft under my head when it was aching most, and, while in a semi-coma, I often saw him bent over me, smiling, though a little anxiously: "Bit better now, isn't it?" And in my stupor I would hear him talking to the dogs, urging them on with the most appalling threats or trying to entice them with fair promises of masses of food when we reached our journey's end. He was always earnest and affectionate with Girly: "Pull now, Girly, pull all you can. We'll get our skipper to land all right."

It was hard sledging all down that dreary coast. Summer had come, and the first half of June was already past; the sun shone bleakly once the wind had hunted the clouds from the sky, but it did have some warmth, enough to be felt at least. The snow melted rapidly and gradually the slush disappeared, leaving clear water lying on the ice and collecting in shallow lakes in all the dips. The ice was rendered brittle by the sun and broke beneath the press of wind and tide. Long channels were formed among the drifting floes, where bright little wavelets glistened gaily and seals broke the surface to turn their bullet shaped heads and watch us with big, round and remarkably expressive eyes. But always they were out of range — worse luck.

One day, during a halt, a bear came. I saw it quite close, but all I could do was to shout to Iver, who was hunting a seal. Then, with considerable difficulty, I managed to cut Grimrian loose from the sledge and hoped that he might keep the bear at bay. But it all went wrong. Grimrian was brave enough when he was one of a pack, but he did not like the idea of going for a bear alone. It would, perhaps, have been a fairly dangerous thing for him to have done; but I, at least, would gladly have exchanged thin little Grimrian for a bear. He began bravely enough, but he changed his mind as soon as he discovered that he was alone, and instead of going for the bear and halting it, sought safety with Iver. Iver dropped to his knee to steady his aim and took a long shot at the fleeing bear. He hit it in the back and wounded it mortally, though without killing it immediately; so, with blood streaming from its wound, the bear dragged itself out to the sparkling water and flung itself in, making the spray spurt up like a golden halo round what could have been our salvation. The bear went down less than a hundred yards from land, watched in amazement by two inquisitive seals who were unable to understand their arch-enemy's strange capers as its life ebbed out.

Bitterly disappointed, Iver sat down by the edge of the land-ice and gazed long at the water, while I, on the sledge, hid my face in my arms. If only I had seen the bear one minute earlier, or if Grimrian had been the dog we had always thought him and not an accursed coward, or if Iver's bullet had struck just an inch further forward — then we could have halted for some days and enjoyed the warmth of the sun, while we ate ourselves back to strength and health on the juicy bear's meat that was now drifting out to sea, and which would have fed our dogs and given them fresh courage and strength.

But that was not to be: instead of rest and enjoyment, the nod I gave Iver meant "We must get on, my friend. We must get to Lamberts Land as quickly as we can, for your sake."

The second cache contained no more food for us than the first, and we wondered more and more. There was some dog food, however, and we were glad for the dogs' sake, perhaps for ours too. During the last couple of weeks, we had shared our pemmican with the dogs, so now they could reciprocate by letting us have a little of their food. But even that hope was dashed, for, however hungry and exhausted the dogs were, they would not eat the strange *ersatz* stuff that dog food was. They just sniffed at it and left it lying, while they roamed round in the hope of finding something better. And they were lucky, for they sniffed out one of the *Danmark* Expedition's meat caches, meat and bacon three or four years old, the stench of which penetrated miles across land and sea. But the dogs liked it better than the artificial product.

Having failed to get the bear and being reduced to only nine ounces of pemmican a day — the largest permissible ration if we were to have any hope of coming through — we could not afford to stop and rest and enjoy what little there was to enjoy — the arrival of summer. Not that that was really so little.

There was a rippling of water on all the mountain-sides; water was rushing in all the beds of the torrents, and greenery was sprouting and growing on the southern slopes. It was lovely. But along the shore, all this rippling water ate great chunks out of the ice and made progress so difficult that a boat would have been a better means of transport than a sledge. The dogs were almost frightened out of their wits, when Iver drove them out into the big lakes that we sometimes had to cross. On occasion, they had to swim in front of the sledges, while Iver pushed from behind and I lay on top of the load being splashed by icy water that cooled my fevered body.

Progress was most laborious, but Iver knew what was at stake and still seemed possessed of Herculean strength, so that he managed it — how, I shall never understand. However, as the slush gradually turned to water and much of it ran out to sea, the going did become a little easier and, before June was out, we sledged into Dijmphna Sound which to us frugal beings seemed a land flowing with milk and honey.

The ice was good for sledging. We passed only a few channels, but seals gambolled and eider ducks frolicked in them, perhaps not in such numbers that you could truly speak of a wealth of animal life, but enough to seem many to us who had certainly not been spoiled where game was concerned. We also saw seals on the ice, on to which they had crawled from the icy water to bask in the warm sun. There were relatively fresh bear's tracks here and there, and gulls were nesting on the mountain-side. The birds left their nests and dived at us or the dogs, uttering shrill cries in answer to Iver's shouts of joy. The dogs recovered their spirits, barking a bit and looking up at the gulls, snapping at any that were particularly obtrusive, and they even began to raise their drooping tails. Snow buntings chirruped gaily on the green land as they hopped from stone to stone. It seemed a good place to be.

It was light all round the clock and, at midnight, the sun shone in the north, a flaming, orange-coloured blaze that lent glowing colour to the dark mountains. It was the northern summer, and we realized that we would have to halt for a short while to let more thaw-water run off the ice, as it must before we could continue. But we also realized that there would be no continuing our journey unless we could get game and plenty of it. Either that, or find the cache the *Danmark* Expedition had made somewhere or other along that coast.

We had no knowledge of what the cache contained. If it only held a few pounds of tinned food, like the two previous ones, it would be of little interest to us, for we had almost no food left and nothing for the dogs except the flesh of one of their number, which we shot immediately when we made camp at this land of milk and honey. If we found the cache, the three surviving dogs would also feel that we believed in, or at least hoped for, better times.

When Iver had pitched the tent and made it as habitable as possible, I was not even able to hobble there with his help, but had to crawl on hands and knees. When I reached it, I collapsed into my sleeping bag, so breathless and giddy with pain and exhaustion that I was convinced that that place was my journey's end. I could go on no longer without, at the very least, plenty of food and a long rest.

As far as I was concerned, it mattered little whether the end came there or a few score miles further on, for I had given up all hope of ever getting back to the ship with its food, rest and, perhaps, medicine to help my scurvy. That hope had been bumped out of me during the many hours when I had lain lashed on top of the loaded sledge, a mere extra burden for Iver and the poor dogs.

Iver and I were quite frank about it all, for I had to explain to him the way he should go, and what he should do in order to have a chance of getting back, when, sooner or later, the dread hour came and he found himself all alone in that vast wilderness.

After all, it was I who had landed him, a man with no Arctic experience, in this adventure, and so I must do whatever I could to get him out of it safe and sound. Every evening I wrote in my journal an account of the scurvy's ravages in my body, and I made Iver promise to take that journal back with him, if it was the only thing he could save, for my description of my illness and its progress would be his only proof that I had died a natural death.

Iver refused to believe that things were as bad as that, and while we camped at Mt Mallemuk, he was out hunting all the time, no matter what the weather, in sunshine and calm, in mist, rain and storm; while I dozed in the tent with a rifle within reach in case a bear came my way, which none ever did. The hours were long while Iver was away, and anxious too, for so much might happen to him.

He could be gone for hours at a stretch, but he never returned to the tent without a hare, a gull, a black guillemot or something. There was not much to be got, for the seals were shy and on the alert, whether they were in the sea or on the ice. What bear tracks he saw were days old, and, though there were many tracks of musk oxen on land, he never caught a glimpse of one, no matter how far he went or how much he searched.

One day he returned sooner than usual and it was obvious that something exciting had happened, for I heard him shouting and yodelling a long way off, but it was not till he was quite near the tent that I realized that he must have found the cache at last.

Beaming with delight, he assured me that it was a big cache, a whole provision case, full rations for two men for a fortnight, an incredible quantity of food for men who were famished. Now we should really be able to eat our fill for several days — if the contents had not been ruined by water which, unfortunately, was possible.

Iver had not opened the cache; he had wanted us to share the pleasure and had just hurried back to me with the good news. He was trembling with excitement as he helped me out of the tent and down to the shore, and he talked incessantly all the time he was harnessing the dogs to the sledge. He sang and laughed as he drove them down to the coast, promising them every imaginable delight. And he kept assuring me that now I should soon get well and fit again, and made me as comfortable as he could on the sledge. "Wait till you see the cache," he said. "It's a splendid sight. That in itself will make you better."

And it was a splendid sight, though perhaps not as magnificent as Iver had made out. Before we ever got there and Iver had opened the tin box, the smell was enough to tell me, who sat waiting on the slope at some little distance, that the contents were not in as good a state as Iver had hoped.

There had been a little hole in the tin box, and water had made its way in, spoiling biscuits and chocolate so that they looked unappetizing and tasted worse. The sugar had melted and some of the tins had rusted through and their contents were far from fragrant. Yet, in our famished state, such a find fully justified our mad joy. We had not seen so much food for ages.

That evening, refusing to heed the admonishing voice of caution, we indulged in a regular feast. Iver received a pound tin of lobscouse as a finder's reward, and, though I would have liked to have had meat, we both thought that porridge would be best for me. The oatmeal was very musty, but we thought it edible; so Iver cooked me porridge, and it smelt almost delicious in our little tent. We ate and enjoyed our meal in devout silence, savouring each spoonful with gusto, and when we finished up with coffee and a piece of mouldy chocolate, we could wish for nothing more.

On such an auspicious occasion, we never gave a thought to scurvy or other infirmities, and, besides, I did feel as though I was beginning to get better. My fainting fits were not nearly so bad; in fact, I had not fainted once since we had rounded Mt Mallemuk and found that lovely camping place. Thus, having a small supply of provisions again and my seeming to be better, we felt that we could look at the immediate future without much anxiety. Luckily, one is optimistic.

The days passed, one like another, and the weather was the only thing that changed. Sometimes it was fine, with high sky and warm sun that lured forth buzzing insects, but mostly it was blustery, raw and misty. Iver was out every day, hunting to get food for his sick companion and in the hope of dropping some bigger game, which would provide meat for the dogs and give us some to take with us when we continued our journey. This, however, he never got, and we had to be content with gulls, not so many as we would have liked perhaps but on the average one a day. It seems that those gulls were what I needed most, for day by day I felt my strength returning, and day by day I could see the livid patches on my body becoming smaller and less blue. As the days passed, I became more and more convinced that the miracle of which I had not dared dream ten days before was actually happening and I was recovering.

We thought we would move our camp nearer to the open water in the hope of getting some bigger game, bear or seal, and, when Iver had struck the tent and I was sitting on the sleeping bag waiting for him to come and help me down to the shore, I had the presumptious idea that I would try to walk by myself.

I scarcely dared try, for it would have been a bitter blow, if the improvement I felt had not really made me any stronger; but in the end I plucked up my courage, heaved myself off the sleeping bag with the help of two ski-sticks, got to my feet with difficulty — and stood, a thing I had not done for over three weeks.

I was so delighted that I threw one of the ski-sticks away, took a couple of steps and then let go of the other, stood for a moment, wavering, without any support, and then took step after step, calling out delightedly: "look Iver, look — I can walk!" Iver's delight was as great as mine. He came hurrying up and wanted to put an arm right round my shoulders to prevent my falling, but there was no need to support me: with a great effort, I kept myself upright and walked right down to the shore and sat down on the sledge, without help.

I believe that so quick a recovery after such a violent attack of scurvy was almost miraculous, nor can I think of any other explanation than the curative properties of the twelve or so gulls that Iver shot out of the sky for me. I ate every particle of meat, sucked down the oil, and even managed to swallow the guts. The meat was hardly cooked at all, for

we had to economize with paraffin as with everything else, and I had to
cut it into tiny bits that I could swallow whole, for my teeth and gums
still ached like abscesses.

On we drove, and each time the sledge stopped I had to get off and
make sure that it was true that I really could stand and walk. Iver and
I were gayer than we had been for a very long time. We sang and we
laughed so that the mountains rang with it, while our three remaining
dogs shared in our elation, raising drooping tails and even wagging
them a little.

Eighteen days after coming to Mt Mallemuk with myself lying on
the sledge half-dead, we left our camp under the high mountain and
went out on to the ice that now was almost bare of snow. I was then
able to do my share of the hardest jobs, and, despite the hard toil and
the fact that our clothes were sopping wet both day and night, I became
stronger every day and was soon as strong as I had ever been. For that
I had to thank my wonderful comrade, Iver, who had toiled superhu-
manly to bring the sledge and me to a place where we could camp for
the summer.

What I admired most, perhaps, and what, after all these years, I still
think of with gratitude and joy, was his continual endeavour to cheer
me up. He always had something cheerful and encouraging to say
when he saw that I needed it. His eyes kept on mine, as he watched to
see whether he could help or mitigate the physical or mental stress that
I was under. I am sure, too, that just as he helped with word or deed
whenever I needed it most, so he never for a second failed me in his
thoughts. And yet he knew full well what my illness and its probable
outcome could come to mean to him, that it could put upon him the
heaviest burden that can be laid on a person's shoulders: the chilling,
paralyzing horror of utter loneliness.

CHAPTER XI

Water and Hunger

Water on the ice — Sledge-boat — Is mildew a vegetable? —
Lack of game on land and sea — Attempt to catch sand-hoppers —
Lamberts Land in sunlight

We had expected arduous conditions on the return journey and we
had had them; but now that I had got rid of my scurvy and was again
fit enough to take what toil and disappointments might await us, we
became over-optimistic. There were again two of us to deal with things,
and we felt that nothing could befall us that would be more difficult to
overcome, than what we had already survived.

It was now summer; the sun was shining and the worst of the water
had run off the ice. With two of us to hunt, we felt that we could not
continue to be as unlucky there as we had been. Now there were two to
share the work and the labour with the sledge, two to back one another
up in any emergency and in the hours of bitter disappointment, two to
do and bear all that which for the last five or six weeks Iver had had to
do and bear alone. Thus, it was no wonder that we were optimistic as we
left Mt Mallemuk and resumed our snail's progress towards the south.
All was well, and we were convinced that the worst was over, for what
lay ahead could not possibly be so hard as things had been, when Iver
was struggling alone and I hung between life and death.

As it was summer, we expected to have to contend with water: there
would be large lakes of thaw water on the ice-floes and broad leads
between the floes themselves; while along the coast, the tides would
have made big fissures in the ice, which would not be easy to cross. On
land, wild rivers would be rushing down from the glaciers of the high-
lands and from the huge snow-drifts melting under the rays of the sun

and yielding masses of water. Things would be difficult; but it should amount to no more than a little delay here and there, and we were well accustomed to that. Besides, we had time in hand, for we had long since resigned ourselves to the fact that we could not possibly reach *Alabama* before she had to leave her winter harbour.

But then there was our other enemy, hunger; that might be really difficult to overcome. We still had a few provisions on the sledge: eight or ten pounds of pemmican, which could be made to go quite a long way, if we ate no more than we had been doing for the last month — half a pound a day. And we also had a few handfuls of biscuits and two tiny tins of tea, the latter our only luxury. But we also had what was of much greater importance than the little food we carried on the sledge, the *Danmark* Expedition's caches further down the coast.

From now on, we knew for certain where those caches were and what they contained, though we had had to travel all the way to Mt Mallemuk to learn this from a letter left for Mylius-Erichsen, which we had found there in the cache. Of course, some of the provisions could have been ruined by water, but there would always be something we could eat. What was edible did not depend so much on the extent to which it was impaired as on how hungry we were. Famished men are not fastidious.

And if everything went wrong and all failed us that we in our excessive optimism felt could not possibly fail, we still had our three wretched dogs; they were thin enough, in fact they were horrible sights, but they must have some flesh on their bones.

All in all, the outlook seemed relatively bright as we left Mt Mallemuk.

We lost much of our optimism, however, as soon as we came out into the fjord and had to spend a long time searching east and west for ways across the many leads that had been sprung in the covering of ice, that before had been so firm. It almost looked as though the ice were in full break-up, a possibility we had never imagined that we need consider.

We had to put on a bit of a spurt if the ice were not to fail us entirely. On we struggled, and one way or another got across the lanes. Often we coolly ferried ourselves on a fragile little ice-floe just large enough to carry the sledge, ourselves and the terrified, whimpering dogs, which hated all that water as much as they had the deep slush.

Only once did one of these ice-ferries fail us, and then it was nearly fatal. Iver was already on the floe with the sledge and dogs, but luckily I was still standing on stouter ice, for all at once the ferry-flow broke into pieces. Exerting all my strength, I was able to hold the front of the sledge against more or less solid ice, while Iver rescued our precious equipment piece by piece. We saved everything that would float, but the rest sank.

Half an hour after the accident we were standing beside a pile of sopping things surveying the damage. Most things we were able to dry; but our mouldy biscuits were done for, though we squeezed the salt water out of them, steeped them in sweet water from a pool on the ice, and tried to dry them over the Primus. The result was not what we had hoped. The biscuits tasted of salt, mustiness and rancid butter, and also slightly of paraffin. It was filthy, but we ate them — and suffered for it for some time. Food must not be wasted, and however dreadful to taste, there must have been some nourishment in them.

The weather was against us. The temperature was above freezing, so that water was simply spouting out of the ice. And then there was the mist, continuous mist that made it almost impossible to find our way through the innumerable leads and channels, all of which seemed to run athwart the direction which we hoped was south — for our one and only compass was one of the things we had lost when the ice-floe ferry collapsed.

Progress was very slow, and this was where we had hoped to be speeding southwards as though with seven-league boots! Our provisions diminished until they were little more than an illusion. The dogs were scarcely able to walk, far less pull, and Girly lay on the sledge unable even to stand, quite exhausted by hard work, hunger and the water. It was pitiful to see.

If only we could have got a bear, all would have changed quickly for the better; but we never did, though we saw lots of tracks along the broad leads, where they had been hunting the seals which gambolled in the cold water full of the joy of spring and gazed at us inquisitively. Iver insisted that he could see them laughing at us and that they deliberately kept just out of range.

Again hunger was tormenting us. The dogs too were very hungry, especially Grimrian who for some considerable time had been practising the art of living on his own and others' excrement. He disdained nothing that was edible — except the salty mouldy biscuits which we had eaten.

We began to talk of shooting a dog to get a little meat and to give the other two dogs some bones to chew on, but we kept hoping for game and let them continue to live and suffer, in the perhaps somewhat vain hope of better times to come.

For some time, I had noticed that Iver kept fingering the dogs when they came to us for solace and comfort, as they did when we stopped to rest, and how, now and again, he would nod thoughtfully to himself after running his fingers searchingly down one of their spines.

I did not understand the meaning of these strange caresses, and was greatly surprised when, in reply to my question, I was told that, though Bjørn was very thin, you could still feel a little fat on him. For a moment I stared at Iver uncomprehendingly, but then I realized what he meant and I was so taken aback that I was just about to curse him for a cannibal, but stopped myself in time, for Girly happened to be on my lap, looking at me with eyes glowing with faithful devotion.

I shrank from the idea, but then I began patting my faithful dog's head with one hand, while the other sub-consciously ran down her spine fingering it, just as I had seen Iver's do on Bjørn.

I could not feel any fat, just the hard vertebrae. Then Iver showed me where he thought he could feel fat and, after that, when the occasion offered, we both unblushingly fingered the dogs' spines and tried to persuade ourselves that there was still a little fat on the poor animals which thought we were caressing them!

There was certainly no fat left on Girly, nor strength either, and she died. It was a miserable reward for all her toil and faithfulness, and for the great ability she had shewn as leader-dog; yet, though I grieved to think that Girly had died of hunger and exhaustion, I was glad that she had died when she did, for that saved me from having to eat the dog I had been most fond of out of all the many sledge-dogs I, as an explorer, had had on my various journeys.

Despite all the water surrounding us, we eventually came to the place where the next cache was supposed to be. Unfortunately, this was guarded by a broad tidal channel, so broad as only to be negotiated in a boat. We constructed one by wrapping all our possessions in the tent and lashing the bundle to the sledge.

First, we experimented cautiously in a shallow lake to see whether the sledge had buoyancy enough to carry the two of us; and having found that, at a pinch, it would, we tied the two dogs to the sledge and pushed off with Iver lying on his belly on the right-hand side, with his legs trailing, and I in a similar position on the left.

There was considerable risk in entrusting ourselves and our goods to such a rickety craft and we were loath to do it; but it was the only means of getting across. We were continuously having to tread water, as the sledge heeled over to one side or the other, but in the end we felt ground beneath our feet and hauled our sledge-boat safely ashore, proud of our invention and our courage — and feeling much more confident about the future. Now we could face smaller stretches of open sea with comparative equanimity. Also we must soon be coming to a cache, where there should be a fortnight's provisions for two men. That was a wonderful thought to us, for all we had left was two pounds of pemmican, a tiny tin of tea and two emaciated dogs, even though Iver insisted that they were not just skin and bone since, as he thought, he could still feel fat on their spines.

We found the cache and suspected at once that all was not well. The tin box was rusted and lying by the waterside, where small waves from the tidal channel could lap over it. It did not look promising, and when we opened it, it was a dreadful sight that met our eyes. Everything that could become mouldy had done so. Things were so covered with mould that you could see nothing else, so thick with cilia that they were like small hairy animals. Some of the tins had rusted through and noisome vapours oozed from the holes.

We turned and twisted the lumps of mould, broke off little bits to see if they were mildewed right through, as unfortunately they were; and we had already decided to scrap all that was mildewed, when Iver suddenly said: "Wait a bit! You've often said that we need vegetables. Isn't mould also a kind of vegetable?"

I doubted whether it was, but it certainly was a possibility, so we cleaned the mildewed lumps of the worst of the mould and ate them. But they did not altogether agree with us.

Nevertheless, there were things there to delight two hungry men. The cache contained enough food for perhaps eight days, if we were careful; and then there was also a full tin of paraffin that we found further up the shore. That was grand, for it meant that we could use our Primus, if we shot anything big — as we soon would — and wanted to fry a steak.

The mountain slopes that faced south were relatively fertile, and we roamed quite far inland in the hope of finding musk oxen in one of the larger glens. These were furrowed by deep river-beds, filled to over-flowing with the milky water that foamed down off glacier and snows and went swirling out to sea.

These torrents were difficult to cross and also dangerous, for we could not see bottom through the milky water and so had no idea how deep they were. Some were so deep that we had to turn with water foaming round our waists and look for another and, we hoped, better ford. The water was also so piercingly cold that the muscles in our legs and thighs contracted into knots of cramp, the pain of which was almost intolerable. However, we would have gladly accepted the cold and the cramp, the pain and the danger, if only the mountain slopes had granted us a sight of the musk oxen which had covered the muddy valley floor with a complicated pattern of hoof marks, shewing where they had wandered to and fro as they grazed themselves fat on the grass and deposited droppings that could not have been old.

There were also considerable quantities of hare's excrement, yet though we walked the country for three days we never saw the white glint in the landscape by which the hare betrays its presence in summertime. Even ptarmigan were so scarce that we only got two to reward us for all our toil in that trackless land of hills and glaciers. After that we gave up. Land animals were apparently even more difficult to see and to get than sea animals.

When, weary and exhausted, we returned to camp after all those hours of fruitless trudging and searching, we saw seals in the tidal channels, but unfortunately they were all so far off as to be out of range. Iver exclaimed angrily. "Do you see that beast out there? God help me, but it's grinning at us." It almost looked as though it was, and we promised to avenge ourselves in the morning.

One night, fortune smiled on us for a fleeting moment. We were roused by an appalling commotion outside, close to the tent: howls and yelps and roars and hisses, and there, a couple of yards from the tent, stood a bear looking in amazement at our two wretched dogs, which were tethered beside the tent door.

We dived for our rifles, but the bear was quicker than we, and by the time we were ready to shoot it had already reached the tidal channel and was beyond our reach, hurrying across the ice in long, low bounds, comical to watch if you were full and satisfied, but a sorrowful sight when hunger was gnawing at your inside.

That was Grimrian's fault. He was so inclined to try and satisfy his hunger by eating rope and gnawing at wood that we had taken our rifles into the tent to protect them from his attentions. If we had not done that — and it was the first time we had — the bear could not possibly have escaped and we would have feasted for many a day. Alas, Grimrian, you little knew what your greed cost you and us that night.

Hour after hour, day and night, we walked to and fro along the tidal channel watching for seal. And we saw seal break the smooth surface of the water, saw the glistening drops of water roll down their round, human heads — we whistled as alluringly as we could, and the seal remained stationary in the water, listening to the unknown sounds, and we took aim with the utmost care and despatched our bullet with a heart-felt wish that this one might at last reach its goal. Each time, however, the seal vanished, seemingly unhurt. We could not under-stand it, for we usually were able to shoot straight. It was conceivable that the rifles had received a bump on the rough journey that had moved the sights; yet when we shot at a small stone as a target, we hit it every time. There was nothing wrong with the sights.

What then was wrong? It was as though the seals were bewitched and impervious to bullets, which we could almost see entering their heads and yet not killing them.

Hour after hour, day after day, we hunted those bewitched animals with the lovely human eyes, and kept sending our bullets across the water at the heads that, in the olden days, made sailors swear that they had seen ferocious mermen, seductive mermaids or other strange creatures that terrified their superstitious minds.

But we never got a seal.

In the end, we solved the mystery, and though it boded us no good, it at least showed that there was nothing supernatural about it: it was simply that the seals did not yet have enough fat on them to keep them afloat after they were shot, so that we were never able to recover them.

I should have thought of that, of course; and so I might, if I had not been too hungry to reason or think clearly. As it was, we did not realize the bitter truth until one day we saw a seal's head actually crushed by a bullet, so that blood and blubber floated on the smooth surface, forming a dirty patch round the seal's head. We were jubilant, for now at last we had got a seal and would be able to eat our fill. But the next moment, our jubilation turned to horror, for the seal floated only for a fraction of a second and then it sank like a stone.

After that we knew, and we also knew that our lives were at stake, for it was obvious that we could not afford to wait for the seals to grow fat. We must, therefore, without wasting time, try to reach a place where we might find land game, or else stake everything on an attempt to get to the next cache, a good seventy miles further south, hoping that it was still in existence.

We were now critically short of food, for all we had left was a little pemmican, one tiny tin of tea and the two dogs, which certainly had not a shred of fat on their thin tortured bodies.

Before we continued on our arduous way, we wanted to try and salvage one of our seals which had sank in some ten feet of water. For a whole day we dragged for it, with no other result than that we became soaking wet and caught some sand-hoppers. That gave us a crazy idea, that we might be able to catch enough to give us a meal of sorts for a day's hard work; so we sacrificed the last bit of Girly for bait, fastening it to a shirt which we lowered into the water, and then carefully watched the sand-hoppers as they swarmed round the titbit. As soon as there were a lot of them within the compass of the shirt, we carefully pulled it up towards the surface, yet, no matter how careful we were, the sand-hoppers always discovered our foul purpose and the next instant were gone. We tried, time after time, but at the end of five or six hours' fishing, all we had got was half a jugful of sand-hoppers, which grated between our teeth and tasted revolting. They had as little effect on our hunger as a snowball on the fires of hell.

After that we gave up fishing for sand-hoppers and made off south-wards with Bjørn and Grimrian securely tied to the sledge, so that there should be no chance of their escaping their ultimate destiny, which was to be killed and eaten.

We struggled on as best we could, toiling till we ached in every joint. We jumped the narrow leads and hauled the sledge over; we ferried across the broader channels on a piece of ice or paddled across, lying on our sledge-boat with our legs in the water. Often we had to jump off into the water and stand on the bottom, to prevent the sledge-boat capsizing.

We managed it, but it was a laborious and appallingly slow business relative to our microscopic store of provisions. We were sopping wet from the moment we started sledging in the evening, until the warm sun stood high in the heavens the next morning and we stopped our all but hopeless labours. Then we wrung the water from our clothes and crawled into soaking sleeping bags to get some sleep, while we waited for the cold of night to lessen the flood of water rushing across the ice and enable us to move on again.

We toiled on across the ice a little to the north of Lamberts Land, where Mylius-Erichsen and Høeg-Hagen had succumbed "twelve miles off the glacier in the middle of the fjord," as Jørgen Brønlund had described it. But there was no glacier wall to be seen there. The inland ice did come thrusting out there, between Lamberts Land and a mountain a little farther north, but it was in an even stream of ice that merged imperceptibly with the sea-ice, so that we were quite unable to identify the spot Jørgen Brønlund had described as "off the glacier." There was no glacier wall. However, when seen in deceptive moonlight, as Brønlund saw it when he left his companions in their last camp, perhaps some eminence in the inland ice had looked like a glacier wall.

Those were just thoughts that occurred to us as we struggled past the scene of the catastrophe in 79 Fjord, almost as near to succumbing as Mylius-Erichsen and his two companions had been. We were starving and exhausted, as those three had been; but where they had been subdued by cold and darkness, we had sparkling sunlight and relative warmth to give us a little hope. That meant a lot; but, on the other hand, we had the water to contend with, and that was bad.

We reached land very near Jørgen Brønlund's grave, and, tired though we were, we went off hunting straight away in the hope of being able to spare one of the dogs. Iver had the double-barrelled shot-gun with shot for one barrel and ball for the other, and I the rifle which could only be used against bear or musk oxen. We went separate ways so as to be able to cover as large an area as possible, and for ten hours I stumbled about that hilly country that was fertile and covered with tracks of musk oxen and hare.

I never saw anything edible, not a living creature. As I was on my way back to the tent, dead tired and my mind paralyzed by the thought that only one pound of pemmican and two emaciated dogs separated us from death by starvation, I heard strains familiar from the relatively merry days, when we were sledging across the inland ice:

> "Why should we sorrow,
> Why let things annoy?
> The world's . . ."

What could have happened to Iver? Probably he had bagged something and was letting his joy resound over hill and dale; yet he had been so peculiar those last few days that I wondered whether the combination of hunger, toil, water and disappointment had not broken his courage and affected his brain. A cold shiver ran down my back at the thought. I had to find out; I had to know the reason for this gay song in the midst of our wretchedness. I yodelled an answer and listened anxiously till Iver replied: "Twelve ptarmigan," and the mountains echoed the cry and flung it back a hundredfold: twelve, twelve, twelve — from mountain to mountain across the whole land.

I felt so weak at the knees that I had to sit down on a stone. I could scarcely believe that fortune at last had smiled on us. To the mind of a famished man, twelve ptarmigan was a mass of meat and meant not only relief, but freedom from hunger. I got to my feet and hurried at a stiff-legged trot across the mountain to where Iver sat on a stone, his face beaming with delight, and in front of him lay twelve lovely ptarmigan — several days' freedom from gnawing hunger.

We were so happy, Iver and I. We wanted to yodel, to awaken the echoes and hear life around us; for the sun was shining and when we got back to the tent, we were going to cook ptarmigan; we would only cook them a little though, we were agreed on that, for to have cooked them properly would have taken too long for people in our state.

But the musk oxen? No, we never saw anything but their tracks, which perhaps were years old. It was also obvious, from the multitude of tracks, that there were hares in those parts, but we very seldom saw one.

You can do very well on ptarmigan, however, provided there are enough of them, and there we had twelve, inconceivable wealth! Iver guiltily confessed that he had gobbled up the bloody head of one of the birds, had thus had something that I had been unable to share. And how we ate! Boiled ptarmigan is tasty, and ptarmigan soup not to be despised. Add to that a jug of tea, and what more could man desire? Nothing. But yes: rest and sleep, and that too we had in more than full measure, for, being relieved of the nervous tension of the last month, we overslept and had to wait almost a whole day before the night's frost made it possible to continue. We made what use we could of the enforced wait by going out hunting again in the sparkling sunshine. This time, the only animals or birds we saw were a hare, which we got, and a flapping snow-owl that we missed.

CHAPTER XII

Things Get Worse

*About dog's liver — Hard alternatives — One good cache and
some not so good — Poisoning — Verbal orgies —
Dreaming of food — Just a little box of tea*

There was certainly nothing to keep us at Lamberts Land, so once more
we tied our two wretched dogs on top of the load and set off, I pulling
in front and Iver shoving behind. We emerged on to the outflow of the
inland ice and had to contend with all the difficulties we now expected
of it: narrow crevasses which we could just get across, or broad gullies
with foaming rivers at the bottom, which were both difficult and
dangerous to cross on ice-bridges that the sun had rendered fragile:
perhaps they would hold, but they might also break, and then! . . .

None broke, however, though we crossed many, but we could never
help shuddering at the possibility of falling in and meeting a certain death
in the swirling icy water beneath. We got off that fearful ice as quickly
as we could and toiled on towards the large island in the south where,
according to the message left for Mylius-Erichsen at Mt Mallemuk, we
should be able to find four or five cases of provisions, if our luck were with
us. That would allow us to stay quietly on the island, the dark mountains
on which appeared so near, though it took us four or five days to reach it.

By the time we got to the island, the last of our tinned food had been
eaten and Iver had shot his dear Bjørn, skinned him, and, as he put it,
made him nicely fit for human consumption. It was nice to be able to
get our teeth into something, but there was not a particle of fat on the
meat, so Iver had been wrong when he fingered Bjørn's back and said
that he could feel fat there. But what about the liver? Were we to eat it
or not? It looked really inviting, yet we had an idea that dog's liver was
poisonous if the dog had died of exhaustion, and we felt that perhaps

the fact that so many of ours had died in the autumn sledging was partially due to the fact that the live ones had eaten the livers of their dead fellows. It was rather a dilemma.

We tried to persuade ourselves that the poison which killed a dog need not necessarily be dangerous to humans, at the worst slightly harmful. We both thought that that sounded logical, yet I was not altogether happy in my mind about it. Then I remembered that there was something about putting a silver spoon into the pot in which anything possibly poisonous was to be cooked, so I got out a little silver frame I always carried on me, prised out the photograph, rubbed the frame till it was shining, and tied a thread to it, so that we could pull it out of the pot to see whether the liver was poisonous or not.

We felt that we really were taking all the requisite precautions, and so we boiled the dog's liver along with the silver frame, and anxiously awaited the result: two pounds of meat is a tremendous quantity when you are nearly dying of hunger.

We must have forgotten something important about colours; but, however that was, when the liver had been cooking for about ten minutes and we hauled the frame out to see what had happened, we found that nothing much had changed, except that the frame was definitely not as bright as it had been, and also it had become slightly brown. The colour, we decided, did not look dangerous, so we agreed that, unless the frame actually turned green, the liver would be all right to eat.

The brown tint grew darker as the liver cooked, but the frame did not turn green, so we ate the liver and patted ourselves on the back at the clever way we had rescued that titbit for our shrunken stomachs.

However, the liver was not as good as we thought, for, shortly after we had eaten it, we fell into a heavy doze and only woke twenty-four hours later, and then with splitting headaches. Thus, despite our precautions, there must have been some poison in poor Bjørn's liver, and we made each other a solemn promise that, when Grimrian's hour came, we would not eat his liver.

There is not much meat on a worn-out, exhausted dog, and what there is does not have a nice taste; but it satisfied us more or less and that was the main thing. However, even with the liver and what we called marrow from the bones, the whole only provided meagre rations for a couple of days, and then it was Grimrian's turn to go to the pot.

Iver shot him, and he had orders to throw the liver into the water at once, so that we should not be tempted. There was something I had to do in the tent, and when I had finished and looked out to see how it was going, I saw Grimrian's skinned body lying on the ice, looking incredibly small and, for the first time, handsome and appetizing, while beside it lay the liver, also washed and appetizing.

I looked reproachfully at Iver, who said that he had just not been able to bring himself to throw that lovely pink food into the sea. Would I not do it myself?

Seeing that he had not done it, I must. Reproaching him for his failure, I walked briskly up to the liver, raised my foot to give it a good kick that would send it far out into the water — and gently lowered my foot again. I then turned to Iver, whose guilty expression had now become rather mocking.

We stood a long while looking at each other and the liver, while we tried to persuade ourselves that this liver, our last piece of edible meat, could not really be harmful. We argued the point to and fro, and that took time, but then Iver produced quite a fresh argument: "Listen," said he, "Bjørn's liver didn't kill us, so Grimrian's isn't likely to either."

There was no contesting that, so we closed our ears to the warning voices of common sense and caution, boiled the liver without the silver frame and ate it. It tasted delicious, but, of course, we should not have eaten it, for it was naturally as poisonous as Bjørn's and had exactly the same effect: twenty hours of sleep and then a splitting headache.

It had other consequences which were considerably worse, but those we did not notice till some days later, but then we really did have to pay for our foolishness and greed.

It was difficult to reach the site of the cache — Schnauder Island, it was called — for there was an infinity of open channels, rushing rivers and thaw-water lakes that we had to cross or ford. We were sopping wet from the moment we began sledging towards the island, to which four cases of food drew us with irresistible force, till we were standing on it with aching limbs and swollen ankles. The latter were the result of slipping and falling on the uneven but glassy ice, and of stepping into the innumerable holes that the thaw had made in the surface, accursed, dangerous holes they were, almost hidden beneath a cover of ice or snow, sometimes as much as knee-deep and just large enough for a foot to go right in.

In the end, however, we reached land, wrung the water from our clothes, flung down the traces and looked at each other interrogatively: What now?

By that time, the last of Grimrian's bones had been scraped clean and smashed to let us get at the marrow, and we did not have an ounce of food left, except for a couple of teaspoonsful of tea. There were only three possibilities: we must either find the cache, shoot something or die of starvation.

We at once set off along the shore, hoping that the cache might be not far away and intact. It was all we could do to stagger along. Iver had pains in his back and side, and his head ached with every step he took. He had been like that for a number of days now. He was worried and so was I, for it would be much worse having to contend with illness then, than it had been when I was sick, bad though that had been.

We were approaching the southern end of the island, and our hopes had dwindled to nothing, when, at quite a distance, we saw a square case on a shoulder of rock, a heavenly sight. We could scarcely walk, yet the sight of that provisions case was so stimulating that we managed to keep going till we reached it. It was as shining and whole as the day it was packed in Copenhagen, five or six years before!

What a joyful moment that was, as we stood in the twilight at that desolate spot, gazing at the tin case that simply shone in the semi-darkness, as though it were illuminated from within by the wonders it contained; a heaven-sent gift for exhausted and famished men. There was immediate solace for all our longings, for inside that case were provisions enough for a fortnight, perhaps a whole month or even longer, if we were as abstemious as hunger had taught us to be. There was all the heart could desire, except rest. Rest we had to have, several days' rest before we could tackle such going again. Iver, in particular, needed it, for he was so thin that he scarcely cast a shadow, so ill that he could hardly stagger along, his face so ravaged that I expected him to collapse at any moment. We must rest for at least a week and gather strength, for there might be a hard time ahead of us on the 300 miles we had still to go before we reached Shannon Island. And the autumn was at hand!

After the first flush of joy, doubt and anxiety raised their heads: there should have been four or five cases, but we had only seen one. Where were the others? We began to search and in the gathering darkness we found the rest of them in a sheltered corner, or rather the remains, for some sledgers had halted there and sampled all the lovely food. How sated and content they must have been! There were plenty of traces of the cache: it had been destroyed by people who had never thought of the possibility that others might come there later, whom the food they ruined might have saved from dying of starvation. The cases had been burst open and the contents scattered far and wide. We searched among the stones and found individual tins with the contents apparently intact, but we found many more which had been split with an axe so that the dogs could eat what they contained: stew, goulash, jam, blood pudding and such things that were never intended as dog food.

It was men from the *Danmark* Expedition who had made the cache to assist Mylius-Erichsen and his companions on their return journey, and, naturally, people from the expedition had every right to use what they liked of their own provisions without accounting to any but their own consciences. And if it could have helped the object of the expedition in any way, they were obviously fully entitled to feed their dogs on food meant for people, even on delicacies — if the dogs would eat them. But the leaders of the *Danmark* Expedition can scarcely have been justified in marking "cache" at various localities on an official map, when they themselves had helped to empty, or almost empty, some of those caches before that map was even drawn. Such a thing could be mischievous. In fact, it all but killed us.

Never, even to ourselves, did we deny that the members of the *Danmark* Expedition could deal with their caches and their contents as they liked, but it was hard for famished men to find all those split tins with mouth-watering labels and to see in the dogs' excrement undigested lumps of slab chocolate or biscuit that had been thrown for the dogs to scramble for and swallowed whole with several layers of wrapping paper, tinfoil and even string.

We hoped that the poor dogs had not had too bad stomach ache or diarrhoea from eating all that lovely chocolate that we would have given a year of our lives to have had; but we felt that they had deserved the difficulties that they must have had in getting rid of the undigested lumps that still lay scattered about the site of the orgy, a sort of corpus delicti, an accusation against a thoughtless man.

It was not pleasant discovering that all that food had been wasted, and it boded ill for what we should find at the other caches; but our delight and thankfulness for that one whole case was so great that we quickly forgot our disappointment and, collecting every bit of food we could find, trudged back through the dark, cold night to the tent, where we sank on to our sleeping bags, exhausted but happy, having sledged without interruption for thirty-six hours.

Iver wrote in his journal: "Never had I thought life so glorious, as when we sat by a little fire eating some of the food we had found, knowing that we had enough for a fortnight!"

How we enjoyed eating! It was not that we guzzled the food. We had been too long without food for that; but we carefully measured out a day's small ration and divided it up into a number of little meals, which we had every few hours. Fortunately, we had also found a tin of paraffin at the cache, so we had no need to worry about fuel.

All was well with us, and we could wish for nothing more. Life was glorious and as full of promise as we of plans for the future.

After two days' rest, I went hunting, while Iver stayed in the tent for one more day. I went out, as though going out shooting, with a ship's biscuit and a lump of brawn in my pocket, and fully convinced that I would be back before long with the quarter of a musk ox bumping on my back. We had seen numbers of apparently fresh tracks of musk oxen on the island, and since that was relatively small, we felt that they could scarcely escape our watchful eyes. Ten hours later, I returned to the tent, disappointed, weary and sore of foot. The biscuit was eaten and the brawn gone without my realizing that I had eaten them.

The following day, Iver went hunting. There was no restraining him, he had to go, and off he went with a lump of brawn in his pocket and just as convinced as I had been that he would get something. Gaily he turned and waved to me before he disappeared. But, many hours later, he returned, depressed and with the same miserable bag as I had had — nothing. We crawled into our sleeping bags, taking pleasure in the sun and comfort from the sight of the food we had found — and determined that now we would rest.

It had now become obvious that we must lie quiet in the tent till we had recovered from the effects of eating the dogs' liver, or at least till these had subsided sufficiently for us to be able to walk without every step causing us intolerable pain, for that was the price that we had latterly been paying for our lack of will power, when the temptation to eat the two dogs' livers had proved too much for us, even though we knew that they were poisonous.

Shortly after eating the second liver, when our headaches had quite gone, our skin began peeling off in great flakes, and wherever our clothes lay close to the body, we developed large, raw sores. The worst, though, was our feet, for the horny skin of our soles broke off, leaving sharp edges which cut like knives into the highly sensitive new skin. Walking became a torment, and we rubbed our sores larger with every step we took.

Our hunting continued to yield no result worth mentioning — for what is a ptarmigan or two to famished men? — so we had to take once more to the ice, with all its toil and thaw-water. Again we had to take our lives in our hands and ferry the sledge across channels a hundred yards wide and more. Fate was kind to us, however. The sledge-boat never once capsized when we were ferrying across the deep places, and though the water chilled us to the marrow, it did not kill us. Thus we stumbled on, on our aching feet, hoping that the sores on our bodies would heal, even though they were still breaking open whenever we moved. But sores do heal, though it takes time, and as the weeks went by, ours also healed and disappeared

The summer was almost over. The cold of autumn set in early that year, and winter sent its grim forerunners across land and sea. The rivers halted their gay summer hustle to the all-engulfing sea, which began to freeze and form a fragile path for us. It was that path that we needed, for if we were ever to get to our journey's end, we must entrust our lives to this thin, but tough, crust that formed on the sea in the raw, cold nights of later summer. But, unfortunately, the first little autumnal storm was enough to break up this thin ice and send it sailing out to the open sea; it needed scarcely more than a breeze, a breath that normally we would have considered nothing at all.

Necessity made us keep going. Our provisions were fast disappearing and, even though we were as sparing as possible, hunger began to make itself felt again. We thought only of food, spoke only of food. We were all too accustomed to danger and hardship and would have taken what came with equanimity — if only we could have got food.

In our thoughts, we relived meals we had eaten in our previous existence, and I told Iver about some of the elegant dinners which I had attended, splendid meals, worthy of a king's table. I listed all the dishes we had eaten, lost myself in descriptions of delicacies that perhaps only existed in my imagination. Sometimes I felt like a cookery book and could almost taste the luxurious things I was describing.

Iver was a good listener. At times a look of amazement came into his eyes, and he grunted, delighted at the thought of some of the dishes I said I had eaten in the distant past, in another life altogether. Now and again, he interrupted me in a description of some especially choice menu to ask if there had not been more straightforward dishes than those I was describing. If we had nothing else, we could at least enjoy the thought of glorious filling food — and feel hungrier than ever.

I also tried to talk of other things, to get away from the verbal gluttony which I had begun. I remember once, when we were passing a moun-

tain, big, tall and long, I gave Iver a little lesson in geology, explaining
how that mountain had come into being in the morning of Time. Iver
listened, drinking in every word, and I was glad that, for a while at least,
we had got away from our everlasting talk of food and fine dinners; then
Iver interrupted and said "Yes, its all very nice and interesting to know
how the mountain came into being, but just think how lovely it would be
if it were made of porridge and we had to eat it all."

That was one way of looking at it!

The thought of food also invaded our dreams, when we were not too
exhausted by the labour of the day to dream at all. The scope of those
dreams was very narrow: Iver usually dreamed of steak swimming in
melted butter, but my dream was more complicated: it was of a large
dish of open sandwiches, but the delicacies themselves were, unfortunately, hidden beneath a sheet of newspaper. The newspaper, of course,
had to be removed, and I was kept busy all night doing so, for each
time I removed a sheet it was only to find that there was another sheet
underneath. In the end there would be tens, hundreds, perhaps thousands of sheets of newspaper piled in a great mountain of paper on my
right, while on my left was the dish, its delicious *smørrebrod* still hidden
beneath yet more newspaper.

When we woke in the morning, with chattering teeth, we told each
other of the orgies we had had in the night, and so the game was on
again. By day we talked about food and by night we dreamed of it;
so that, all round the clock, we thought of nothing but food, and only
fleetingly of the risk we were taking to reach it.

It was not always easy to divide our tiny ration of food with absolute
fairness; but if we had delicious pemmican in the pot, there was no
difficulty, for when the solemn moment came when we considered that
it had cooked long enough, we served it one spoonful to Iver, then one
to me, till the pot was empty. Sometimes, there was a residue left on pot
and lid, and then Iver would lick the pot and I the lid, and the next time
I would get the pot and Iver the lid, and always these were left clean
and bright. We never overlooked the least speck of food.

For a long time, the only "luxury" we had had was tea. We had only a little, half an ounce perhaps, left in the little box, and this was produced on solemn occasions of especial rejoicing or to cheer us up at times of great adversity, such as when our provisions were so low that we had to content ourselves with hope.

One day, or rather night, I was awakened by the effect of having drank a great deal of water the day before, which we had done in order to have something inside us to help make our stomachs feel full. That avenged itself now in the middle of the night. Getting out was not pleasant, for it was bitterly cold outside the clammy warmth of our sleeping bags; but we had learned how to avoid that: an empty food tin was excellent for the purpose and one always stood by our side. That night, after my orgy of water, I made use of my tin, and just as I lay down to sleep again, I heard a plop, but I paid no attention to it; for it was probably just one of the many different sounds the ice is able to make.

When I woke, I discovered to my horror that the little box of tea that had given us so much comfort, was not in its place. I was certain that the evening before it had been standing on the cooking box near my sleeping bag, but eventually I discovered it at the bottom of the tin that had relieved me of my distress some hours before. I looked across at Iver: he was sleeping as though he would never wake, so, knowing what tea meant to us both, I fished the little box out, poured off the superfluous, foreign fluid and squeezed as much as I could out of the leaves, which I then dried, more or less, on my body — all before Iver woke.

That morning Iver badly wanted tea, but I said that there was so little left, that we had better wait till the toil of the day was over; and perhaps we might find game before evening came. Iver sighed and admitted that I was right; but his face lit up that evening when I made tea for us both and gave him his share. I was rather anxious about how the tea would taste, but I soon realized that it was by no means a bad brew. I could scarcely detect any unwonted flavour, though I knew it must be there, and Iver just said, in a happy tone of voice: "What a good thing that, at least, we still have a little tea."

That, too, was what I thought, and I was glad that I had kept my mouth shut about the night's little accident.

We used those leaves again and again, until we could squeeze no more taste or colour out of them; and how poor and how forlorn we felt, when we had to do without the blessing of tea!

Years later, I told Iver what had happened to the little box of tea, and all he said was that it was a good thing I had done what I did, for without tea, no matter in what state, things would have been even more difficult to endure.

CHAPTER XIII

The Days Shorten

*Autumn overtakes us — Open sea — We abandon the sledge and
our sleeping bags — Following the shore — Storm, cold, hunger —
We leave our diaries in a crack in a rock*

When we were in Danmarks Fjord, we often wondered what sort of a
state we would be in if we did not reach the ship before summer overtook
us. We had thought — and feared — that it would be more than difficult
to get through the summer, if we were forced to spend it on the coast, and
still have strength enough left to defy the harsh days of autumn. After all,
Mylius-Erichsen and his two companions had not managed it.

Far into the summer, we were still talking about the menace of
"summering" and shuddering at the thought, until one evening, as we
sat in the tent talking about it, we suddenly realized that there was
nothing to discuss or fear — we had done it! The summer was, in fact,
over, for the sun had gone below the mountains at midnight and it was
then dark in the tent.

Of course, it was not the first time we had noticed that it grew dark at
night; but it had come so gradually that we had never stopped to think
about it. It was not till we found that we needed a piece of candle so as
to be able to see to repair some skin shoes, that it suddenly came to us
that we had got through the summer.

Iver was quite bewildered by the discovery. Then he smiled and said,
"Well, we've got through the summer, and more easily than you thought
when we talked about it in Danmarks Fjord."

He was right. Things had gone better than I had thought possible.
Although we had every reason to fear what the autumn might bring,
we were as happy and satisfied as it is possible to be with worn equipment, clothing in rags and only food for four or five days' very careful

consumption. And, of course, we could never quite forget that we still had the best part of two hundred miles to the nearest proper shelter, the hut at Danmarks Havn.

The nights became long, cold and dark. The stars sparkled and twinkled; the Northern Lights flickered yellow, red or green across the dark night sky, flaring up so that they almost extinguished the stars, or fading until they could scarcely be seen, were no more than a hint, a fire smouldering in space and ready to break out again, a continual play of light, movement and colour.

Autumn had now come in earnest. All water had disappeared from land and ice, and the sea was covered with new ice, which felt good and relatively solid, though we still listened to the ring of the runners and to our own footsteps: if the sound was clear and sharp, then all was well; but if it was woolly and blurred, then we had to be very careful, for the ice might easily be too thin.

You must never expect too much in the North; and even when you are most confident of success, you must never forget that the evil spirits of the polar lands possess powerful means for hurting those who boast that they have overcome all the mischief those lands can do.

It is not always easy to remember this, and while the sledge slid easily over the ice and we made good progress, Iver and I told each other proudly that, despite all our bad luck, things had not gone so badly after all. And, though we never said so aloud, we both thought that we were a rather wonderful couple and other things, such as you can think of yourself when your belly is not quite empty and Fortune seems to be smiling slightly on two foolhardy humans.

But there was a skerry further on and there sat a grim evil spirit, who knew much better and laughed treacherously at the two wretched little creatures who had such good opinions of themselves and even thought that they had outwitted mighty, merciless Nature by their own strength and courage and ingenuity, and that it was themselves they had to thank for having got as far as they had. Thus, when after some hours' easy sledging across the shiny new ice, we set foot on the skerry and threw down the traces to storm up to the crest, happily anticipating that we should see the sea to the south covered with ice as good for sledging as that we had just been crossing, our gay, expectant voices roused this evil spirit and he blew his icy breath on us, sweeping all our arrogance away and shattering our faith in the future, like the ice on the puddles we had crushed as we stormed along, hurrying to see good ice between the skerry and the mainland, twelve miles or so to the south. When we reached the top and looked towards the south, our eyes were dazzled by the sunlight glinting on the capricious little waves of an entirely open sea, and we heard a slight swell running, sighing and lamenting up and down the beach.

We stood there, silent and rigid, as if the sight of all that water had turned us to ice and paralyzed thought. As far as our eyes could reach towards the east and south, where lay our way to Danmarks Havn, 120 miles distant, there was not one piece of ice to be seen, not the smallest floe.

After an hour's anxious searching, however, we found a way we could go, though it meant taking a risk that no-one in his right senses would have taken. To the west of us was swaying new frozen ice and across this we made our way, treading most delicately, till we found ourselves standing on the same land as Danmarks Havn. If our strength held out and we neither of us broke a leg on the way overland, neither ice nor water could now stop us reaching the hut.

We could have done with some provisions to help maintain our strength, but, instead, we were compelled to tighten our belts still further, for the first cache we reached after defying the evil polar spirits was empty. Tins that had been chopped open with an axe told all too plainly what had happened, and again we saw how heavy slabs of chocolate and life-giving oatmeal had been thrown to dogs. We searched among the stones and turned over every tin we saw, but we found nothing we could eat. What man or dog might perhaps have left had been destroyed by storm and moisture.

There was no time to spend on pointless wondering what could have induced people to treat food in that way. What had been done could not be undone, and now, having combed the empty cache, we realized that the final spurt overland to Danmarks Havn was going to be the hardest part of the whole race. It called for travelling light, hard and swiftly, so we decided to abandon the sledge and everything that was not absolutely vital.

The tent that had been our home for six months, and in which we had spent so many hours, happy, sad or in anxious waiting for something to turn up, was itself too heavy to carry. We must do with less, so, resolutely, we cut it into pieces and each took just as much as would cover us. Our sleeping bags were also too heavy and were cut down to mere foot-muffs. We left one rifle with a few cartridges at the empty cache, and so, with just the absolutely essential and our diaries in a bundle on our backs, we set off southwards along the shore.

We followed the line of the coast, half-heartedly rejoicing when we came to a stretch of beach on which we could walk more or less normally, and being mildly annoyed when the mountain rose almost perpendicular out of the sea and we had to make our way, clinging by our hands to the sheer rock face, with sardonically chuckling and not unattractive little waves three feet or so away. Or we stumbled apathetically across a foreshore in which were innumerable deep holes and pitfalls between a chaos of huge boulders, which we could only cross by jumping from one to the other. That was dangerous, so dangerous that time and again we thought longingly of the crevasses of the inland ice and of the three feet of slush or thaw-water on the sea-ice. They had been hard and difficult enough, but these boulders were worse, much worse than anything we had experienced so far. And now we were starving into the bargain, and no longer steady on our feet; we slipped easily and stumbled still more easily — in fact, it was a miracle that we negotiated that boulder-strewn foreshore without breaking a leg.

We walked on and on until we could go no further, then we lay down behind a stone, thrust our legs into our foot-muffs, cooked a lump of pemmican and gave the paraffin can an anxious shake: there was not much left. And so we tried to sleep despite the piercing cold, and lay there shivering most miserably and just longing for enough daylight to be able to stagger on again.

And then we saw a bear just ahead of us on the foreshore, where it had been feasting on a freshly caught seal. Unfortunately, the bear also saw us, hissed, growled angrily and walked off towards the sea, began to run, was hit by a bullet in the back, reached the water and splashed out into the sea to die twenty yards from land and far beyond our reach.

We sat down on a stone and gazed dully at all that meat and fat that could have fed and warmed us for days, perhaps weeks, if only . . . But the current was carrying the bear out to sea and we shook our heads resignedly. Our hopes all tumbled round us and the instinct of self-preservation was the only thing we had to help us: we must carry on or die. We got to our feet and, cold and exhausted, staggered about among the stones to see if the bear had overlooked a bit of seal that we could eat. There was nothing but a piece of gnawed lung, and so we walked on in silence, till weariness toppled us and we sought rest in a bed of stiff-frozen moss.

We followed the coast into the mouth of a fjord with skerries, where, from higher up, we had seen practicable ice stretching across to the opposite coast. But clouds were piling up over the mountain tops in the west and rolling down their black sides. Those were threatening signs, and if the weather turned to storm, the ice ahead of us, our way to salvation, might easily break up. If it did, it might be days before it became practicable again, or else we would have to walk round the fjord, adding a hundred miles or so to the distance, and that we were incapable of doing.

We had one stroke of luck, however, for we shot four ptarmigan, fat ones by the feel of them, and good to have in reserve, since we had dreadfully little pemmican left and no paraffin to cook it by. It was bad having no paraffin but, as usual, "It is an ill wind." Having no paraffin, we had no need of a paraffin tin, which, accordingly, was left there on the beach. The now superfluous Primus went the same way, as also a casserole, and that lightened our loads. When pleasures are few, they call for little in the way of equipment — and how grateful one is!

We walked along the land as long as the light lasted, hurrying as much as we could in an attempt to race the gathering storm, which won, despite our efforts, and fell upon us in a scurry of snow, driving us to shelter behind a boulder where we lay for a day or two until it subsided.

The ice was still bearing then, and it was with comparatively easy minds that we walked out on to its even surface. This we found covered by a thin layer of snow, which made walking easy and helped us to keep our feet when a squall came sweeping down from the interior to remind us that, though one storm had passed, there were others gathering where it had come from. However, we could no longer consider what might be coming; we had to press on, and if a storm came, then it made little difference whether it struck us down on the ice or took us out to sea on a floe it had detached, or if we died of hunger and cold on land.

So we walked on, walked and walked across the thin ice towards some skerries that lay in our path, half way to the coast in the south where we would be saved.

We reached the skerries and sat for a while behind a stone to get our breath and recover from the effort, rejoicing in having got roughly half way across the fjord. If the ice was bearing further on, we should be on the same land as the food in Danmarks Havn before nightfall. Our imaginations conjured up visions of food, and we stilled our hunger with the only means we had: talking about food, a veritable orgy of food-words.

Stiff-legged, chilled to the marrow and starving, we struggled against the wind to the top of the skerry in order to get a view of the ice towards the south. What we saw was water, open sea reeking with frost-haze and spray whipped up by the violent squalls.

There was nothing to be done, absolutely nothing. We had to wait where we were. Despite cold and hunger. Was that skerry to be our journey's end, or would we be given yet one more chance?

We found a miserable shelter in a little cleft in the rock, and there we sat huddled for two or three interminable days. We crept as close together as possible, or lay clasped in each other's arms for the sake of the warmth, first chest to chest, then back to back. We tried to draw the greatest possible warmth from each other's icy bodies, hoping thereby to thaw our limbs. Or was it that we merely felt a relative warmth, because we hugged so close that the icy wind could not slip in between us? When the cold became too biting, we stamped a little warmth into our bodies, staggering up to the top of the skerry to see if we could not soon venture on to the ice again. But each time the storm was still driving clouds of frost-haze across black storm-whipped water, and we crawled disappointed back into our shelter and lay there thinking of food. Iver wrote in his diary:

> We never get anything warm inside us now, for we have no fuel. And here on the island there are no willow twigs or anything else that will burn, which is a great pity, as we still have a little tea left!

It was a pity! And that sentence also ended Iver's journal for that part of the journey, for when the storm at last blew itself out and the frost healed the wounds the waves had torn in the ice, so that we could stagger on towards the coast in the south and the food awaiting us at Danmarks Havn, we left behind on the skerry even the few things we had brought so far. Wrapped in an old shirt and stuffed into a crack in the rock, beneath a stone so that no storm could scatter the contents, lay our diaries, Mylius-Erichsen's reports, plus every one of the few things that a week previously we had thought essential for the mere maintenance of life!

The sea we were now to cross was covered with a shiny film of ice; we no longer bothered whether it was thick or thin, would bear or not. We had to get on, if we were not to die of hunger and cold on that desolate skerry. But though we could risk our own lives in walking the twenty miles or so to the land in the south across extremely thin ice, we dared not risk our papers by taking them with us. If we did not get across, there remained a possibility that our diaries in the crevice in the rock on that skerry might be found, and our journey and death thus not have been altogether in vain.

It was a wrench leaving the diaries behind, our record of every gleam

of sunshine that had encouraged us, or of each bitter piece of bad luck
we had encountered. We knew, though, that if we got across the ice
all right and reached land in the south, then sooner or later we would
retrace those miles to the north and fetch the bundle, that we had left
on a skerry one autumn day when our lives hung in the balance.

CHAPTER XIV

The Last Spurt

On the same land as Danmarks Havn — Hallucinations about food and warmth — The temptation of a sunny valley facing south — Rest and sleep behind a boulder — Fear of the rifle — We nearly freeze to death — A small tin of soup — Under a roof at last — Food, lots of food

We left the skerry, that place of cold and hunger, and miraculously got across a tidal break with water bubbling in our tracks. Then we set off walking and walked on and on across the smooth ice, on whose mirror-like surface the rays of the midday sun were sparkling and playing straight into our eyes. That had a strange hypnotic effect. We no longer spoke, did not even think, we just saw the flickering light and heard the dull tread of our feet on the smooth thin ice as something far away.

We walked on and on, and though the coast in the south still seemed as far away as ever, we knew that we were bound to reach it, if we could only keep going and the ice held. So we walked and walked, not even thinking of food or aware of hunger — the end of our hardships was in sight: either in a few bubbles and a small hole in the ice, or we would reach the ever-receding coast.

The ice held and, after many hours of automatic walking, the coast suddenly took to coming towards us in great bounds. We saw huge boulders around us and before we properly realized what had happened, or how, the twenty miles lay behind us and we stood on the same land as Danmarks Havn and food.

We sat down on a stone and shook hands. We did not say much, for words were no longer necessary between Iver and me. We bowed our heads in thankfulness, sat quite still for a while, capable of thought once more, though without conscious control of what we thought. Our minds felt so strangely empty after the great effort, yet among our rambling thoughts there was still room for gratitude for our deliverance that day.

When the sun went down behind the mountains and the full moon rose up out of the sea in the east, we pulled ourselves together, for we had to get on. So, up with you, Iver, and on we go. And now we must just walk on and on and on, and we'll soon come to food.

Food, however, was still sixty miles away, so we just had to endure and walk, go on walking till we could no longer set one foot before another, then sink down behind a stone and sleep till the cold woke us, and then walk on again, walk until weariness overcame the will to walk even to save our lives.

We staggered along through bright moonlight and raven-black shadows, and we were still stumbling along the coast the next morning, when the sun broke through the frost-smoke in the east. But then we could go no more. There remained just one more bit across a little glacier — a last obstacle that nearly became *the* last, for the glacier had a large, mirror-like surface that sloped down to the black sea, and on this we slipped; fell, caught hold of small protuberances, got to our feet, slipped again, and each slip or tumble brought us nearer the black and smoking sea. But we got across the glacier, and, steaming with sweat in the icy air, we collapsed behind a stone and slept till the cold ran icy barbs deep into our bodies and woke us.

The coast beyond that glacier was luckily low and easy going, so we staggered along, as well as we could, while hunger gnawed at our vitals and the thought of food never left us.

Suddenly I found myself thinking of all the white packages of sandwiches that used to lie on the shelves outside the classrooms when I went to school. I could see them, smell them and then I began to count them, ten, twenty, thirty. Then something obtruded on the hallucination and I actually saw a packet of sandwiches, just one, but a big one, lying on the shore a little to the right of me and not far away.

I thought: you must hurry, else someone will pinch it before you get there. And I turned aside and began hurrying towards it, when a surprised question from Iver brought me back to the bitter reality of a desolate beach on the coast of the polar seas, where a little white stone lay glistening in the sunlight.

It was a lovely vision, and I would have gladly enjoyed it a little longer whatever the cost.

Iver was in no better state than I, for where I saw modest packets of sandwiches, he saw whole cases of food. He just gave his head a despairing shake each time he stubbed his tender feet against what was just a stone.

All at once Iver was walking at my side saying something about a green valley that faced south. The beach was stony and we could not help bumping into each other, and as I was interested only in food and not in green valleys, I told Iver to drop astern, explaining that it was impossible to walk two abreast on that ground and in our state.

Shortly afterwards Iver again appeared at my side, and I told him quite roughly to drop behind:

"'Either you go first, Iver, or I do; we can't have the comfort of walking side by side, that will get us nowhere."

Iver sighed and dropped behind, but he came up alongside time and again, until I said:

"What is it, Iver? We can't walk together. You can see that." He tottered as he stood on his tender, aching feet, so we sat down on a stone. "What's wrong with you, Iver?"

"Nothing," he said, shaking his head. "It's just that I'm so tired. And then I keep thinking about that lovely, little valley up there in Skaer Fjord. You remember it, don't you? It faced south and caught all the midday sun."

Yes, I remembered it. "But what about it?" I asked. Iver sat and thought for a while before he replied:

"I am so tired, and I would like to lie down, and I thought! . . ."

He had no need to say more.

Then I spoke harsh words to my good Iver, threatened to use what force I could, if he did not give up that idea. And I told him about the bodies I had seen of men frozen to death along the trail through the gold lands of Alaska. They too had been tired and had just wanted to rest for a moment. They too had had a sunny valley before their eyes, but no companion to drive them on. And so they died, Iver, frozen to death while they dozed from sheer weariness. Do you want to do the same, now that we are so near our objective? Do you want to lie down and die in your green valley — and leave me alone?

No. Of course he did not, but it had done him good to talk about it, and so had the rest, short as it was, and the appeal to his sense of comradeship perhaps most of all. I only know that before long we were staggering on, I in the lead, Iver behind, while I kept looking over my shoulder to make sure that he was not straying off into his green valley.

Hours passed and night fell, so that we could no longer see to walk. Fate, however, was kind and there was a dead calm, so that though the cold was piercing, we were able to get a couple of hours' restless sleep, before we laboriously got going again, just as the first flush of morning began to glow on the peaks of the mountains far inland.

We were no longer so aware of our hunger, I suppose because we were too weary and tortured to be able to distinguish an individual lack or pain, where so many dulled our senses. Iver suffered more than I, because he had rashly bathed his sore feet in a brook with rippling water, and had got a lot of sharp grains of sand between his toes. He had done that three days before, and the sharp sand had now chafed the skin off his toes, leaving them raw and bloody, so that he suffered dreadfully as we walked — on and on and on.

Now and again, however, hunger did come to the surface and drive all other sensations from our consciousness: we felt it then as a physical pain, an overwhelming desire for food.

Again Iver came up alongside me, and for some minutes we walked in silence close together, swaying on our feet, stumbling and bumping shoulders; it was impossible to continue like that. "Either behind or in front, Iver, I don't mind which; but we can't walk close together, however much we would like to."

Iver dropped behind and I could hear his unsteady footsteps on the frozen ground, his occasional stumbles over a stone, his grunts when the pain became too great to be borne in silence. Then there he was alongside me again.

When this had happened several times, I halted and we sat down on a stone.

"What is it Iver?" I asked. "Is it the valley again?"

He did not say much. He just sat and stared out into the distance and shook his head: "No," he said, "it isn't the valley. I'm famished, I can't do much more."

I too was famished and not able to do much more; but there was nothing to be done about it. We had food in Danmarks Havn and there was no chance of anything edible before that, unless we ran into a bear and could shoot it.

Shoot? I looked at Iver, who was carrying the rifle, and a thought came into my head: "Tell me honestly, Iver: is it the rifle you are afraid of?"

He nodded despairingly, looked at me steadily and held out the rifle: "Take it and give me something of yours to carry. I can't have the rifle any longer — it's dangerous."

So then I knew, and I refused to carry the rifle: "Keep it, Iver," I said, "carry it as you have been doing and don't think too much. But if it will help your peace of mind, I can tell you that I see you in front of me the whole time. And when hunger dulls pain, weariness and reason, my thoughts are no doubt the same as yours: if he should drop and die, what then? Will you, or won't you, eat a bit of what is no longer Iver?"

Iver nodded assent and said: "Yes, but I've got the rifle."

"I know that, Iver," I said. "But keep it. After all our struggles we can walk on together, till we can walk no farther; and we can struggle on together, till we can struggle no more — or have come to our journey's end."

And so we stumbled on, I in the lead — searching out the smoothest way between the stones, snow and ice, and Iver walking behind me with the rifle slung on his back, both of us struggling with such ghastly thoughts as only those who are mortally tired, starving and tormented can fall prey to.

We were no longer sure where on the coast we were, and kept thinking that we saw land we knew ahead of us: there surely were the two small hills of Seventeen-kilometre Headland, the outermost headland in the south? When we got there, it was not Seventeen-kilometre Headland after all; but a little farther on we thought that we could distinguish in the gathering darkness the two small hills of — Seventeen-kilometre Headland.

Night fell. Darkness enveloped us and made everything appear unreal, concealing stones and streams and ice from us. We stumbled, fell, slipped, staggered on till we reached a huge boulder that broke the slight current of air from the north, offering two weary men a place to rest and warmth of a sort in 20° C below zero.

The moon had not yet risen and, not being able to see to continue, we had to halt, and so we lay down to rest, sleep and collect a little strength for the last lap. I fell asleep at once and had a lovely dream: I was at home in my parents' house with my back to a glowing tiled stove, and in front of me stood my mother with a dish of sandwiches saying: "Eat, my boy, you must be hungry after that long tramp." I looked at all that lovely food, listened to Mother's voice and enjoyed the heat that was almost scorching my back. All was well, and I was at peace with myself, but I was slightly annoyed by someone who kept saying: "Come, let's go!" Why should I go, when I was so comfortable? It was a crazy idea. But then I heard the voice again, and now it was Iver's voice. He shook me by the shoulder and said: "Come, let us go, or I'll freeze to death."

Then I was awake. The moon was just over the horizon in the southeast, big and round and red. It was bitterly cold, and the wind had veered and was blowing straight on to my back and making it burn — not with the heat of the stove of my dream, but with searing cold. With Iver's help I got to my feet, stood there swaying while Iver fixed the knapsack on my back, telling me with chattering teeth of the fearful pain he had in his feet. And so we tottered on by moonlight and saw the sun rise, half veiled by frost-smoke. It was fearfully cold.

Then we saw the two hills again, but now there was no doubt: this was Seventeen-kilometre Headland.

And then we found food!

It was a tin of Beauvais soup, left behind by the lavish men of the *Danmark* Expedition, the smallest size of tin there is, but to us a thing of splendour, hope of remaining alive, an irrevocable promise that at last the worst was over.

Carefully we opened the tin with a sheath knife and made a little fire with pieces of packing case, some rich man had flung there. And so we had food again, almost scalding food — after I do not know how many days. Devoutly we snuffed in the glorious smell of soup, and felt the magic life-restoring stuff trickle down our gullets and reach to the uttermost fibres of our bodies. The sun was shining and the smoke from our modest little fire rose straight up to heaven, a thank-offering, accepted by God.

From there we had only eleven miles to more food, lots of food, much more than the small tin of soup that had put such life into us. So we laughed to each other with mouths that had almost forgotten how, and talked with lips that were cracked by the frost, stiff and hard from having been pressed together so long as we struggled.

We had to get on. We had to cover those last eleven miles and reach the hut before darkness fell and halted us. We could not stand another night without warmth and shelter. So we helped each other to our feet, our feet that hurt as though we were treading on red-hot iron, and laboriously staggered on. Then we left the endlessly long coast and turned inland, up towards the green ridge behind which lay the *Danmark* Expedition hut.

We put our arms round each other's shoulders and walked till we could walk no more; then we rested a short while in the warming sunshine, till we noticed that clouds were blowing up from the west giving warning of storm, and the instinct of self-preservation forced us to our feet again. A storm then would have meant our death.

We saw the hut from the crest of the hill. It was small and tumble-down, but to our eyes a palace. So we tottered on downhill towards the goal that we had seen in imagination so often on our long journey.

Again and again we had to rest, the last time only fifty yards from our goal, the hut which to us two starving and exhausted wayfarers meant food and days of rest.

When I stood up to walk those last fifty yards, Iver could go no farther. He sat where he was and asked me to come back with a biscuit, a piece of chocolate, no matter what, as long as it was something to eat. I nodded to say that I would, but when I fell, rather than walked, into the hut, I forgot all about my friend Iver who sat waiting out there longing for food, for there on the table in front of me lay a packet of chocolate, and it drove all other thoughts from my head. With trembling hands I tore the covering apart, and then I ate. Oh, how lovely it was!

Iver came staggering in on his own, however, and sank down on a bench by the table. Without saying a word I shoved a slab of chocolate across to him, and he munched it up with much smacking of lips and grunts of pleasure.

Then, for the fiftieth time at least, I began to impress upon Iver — and myself — that we must be very careful with food and not be too voracious to begin with, for to overeat could be dangerous. I told Iver that at home, when a man was so weak from starvation that he had to be taken to hospital, they gave him nothing but spoonfuls of chicken soup.

Weak from starvation? We knew what starvation was, if anyone ever had and survived. And we promised each other to be very circumspect, to eat little and often; we were going to be really sensible.

We forgot all about it, of course; reason was quite unable to keep us from food, now that we could have as much as we liked. Before long a fire was burning in the little stove, and when some hours later, we stretched out delightedly in warm, new sleeping bags and could look forward to a long, undisturbed sleep, we had each eaten a pound of chocolate, a lot of porridge, at least a pound of stew, drunk a pint of cocoa which we had not been able to make thick enough, and eaten endless biscuits and butter piled with sardines. It had been heavenly!

But the paradise of the hungry proved the hell of the sated.

However, the violent shock of that great meal did not strike us dead as we deserved, and gradually we got our appetites so well under control, that we only ate what we needed. It is possible that any reasonable person would have considered what we thought a modest ration, astounding gluttony; but then we were not quite like — reasonable people.

CHAPTER XV

Winter Again

In Danmarks Havn — We attempt to fetch our diaries — Southwards
towards Alabama — We reach Shannon Island — The ship wrecked —
Alone in North-east Greenland — The second winter — An evil dream

We ate and we rested in Danmarks Havn and let our wounds, both
physical and mental, heal. We revelled in the security of a house that
stood on rock and was fairly well supplied with food and fuel, and in the
snugness of it, when the storms of autumn swept across the land and the
snow drove past the little hut in great, blinding clouds. We rejoiced in the
still, fine days and in the crackling frost, which we hoped would throw
a bridge between us and our companions on Shannon Island, for we had
already had enough of open water and thin ice, more than enough, and
we had no wish to be exposed to it again.

We talked now of the day that could not be so distant, when we
would pull our sledge into the little haven and up to *Alabama*, which we
so ardently hoped might be lying safe and sound in the winter harbour
for a second year. We hugged that hope, and soon felt almost convinced
that the ship must be there. That conviction grew and grew, so that
before long we felt quite sure that the ship was still at Shannon Island
with our companions on board, even though I myself had given orders
that she was to sail by August 15 at the latest. We were now well into
September, yet when we talked of the ship, it was not with a doubtful
"*if* she is there," but with a convinced "she *is* in the haven, as we left her,
and the others are waiting for us."

Hope so easily turns to certitude, when you wish something very
strongly, and are alone, and for months have had nothing but that hope
to which to cling. And we hoped greatly, and rejoiced greatly, and the
days were lovely that we spent in the little hut on the plain behind

Danmarks Havn, with plenty of food and enough fuel for our modest needs.

For a long time the instinct of self-preservation had allowed us no respite by day or night, but now that we had reached safety, it had temporarily lost its hold upon us, while the voice of duty became proportionately more urgent and obtruded itself upon us at the most inopportune moments. That was a voice that could not be ignored, for it spoke to us admonishingly about the diaries we had left behind on the skerry, telling us that we ought at once to retrace those seventy miles to fetch them. Then only would we be able to rejoice unreservedly in having come through.

Yes, those diaries! If only we had had them with us! The thought of them plagued us by day and even in our sleep at night. It depressed us to think that we ought then to be sledging north towards the swiftly increasing darkness, with its storms and driving snow so thick, that we would have to stumble blindly along, just in order to fetch them. It was what we should have been doing, and what we had to do before the weather became too frightful and the snow too deep: we must pay to the full for having given way to panic and left our diaries and observation journals in that fissure in the rock.

So we made a little sledge, no heavier than what we thought we should be able to pull when it was loaded, and we made a tent just big enough for two. Then we set about packing provisions for the trip north, and as we did that, we also fulfilled the more pleasant task of packing others for the next and last trip of the year, that would cover the last 130 miles to the ship and our companions.

For just under a month we rested and recruited our strength for the journey north, and then, with traces across shoulder and chest, we struggled up and across the crest to the east of the hut, down to the sea ice and up along the coast towards the sinister darkness and the winds and drifting snow. The sledge that had seemed quite light at the hut, now felt as heavy as if it were loaded with stones. The tent was also heavy and not at all snug, and the going was appalling. When, after seven days, we had only covered about an eighth of the distance, we had to abandon the idea of getting to the skerries on that occasion, even though it meant a much

longer journey in the spring. We could endure no more; so, making a
virtue of necessity, we turned and retraced our steps with a strong following wind and snow at our backs. Thus, for the second time, we reached
the little hut at Danmarks Havn and found shelter from the unruly
weather, that was ushering in the winter and warning all live things to
get to their dens and there wait for better times.

We, though, were not like the beasts of the earth, who could wait for
better conditions; we had to try another bout with darkness and storm,
for we must get back to the ship and the others and to all the glorious
things that awaited us there, for in Danmarks Havn there was neither
food nor fuel enough to last the whole of the long winter.

So we loaded our sledge again, nailed up the door and set off, heading
for the light in the south. At noon that part of the sky was still golden,
and in the middle of that golden patch lay *Alabama*, 130 miles away.

We grew tired and breathless after only a few hours' toil with the
sledge; our legs ached and it was devilish hard to get along. We had
to have frequent rests, but it was the last journey for that year, and
when it was over we would have reached the ship and the others, so
we must not waste time with too much bewailing and resting: "Come
on, Iver, on again! We two have overcome much worse than this."
So we picked up the traces once more, flung ourselves into them and
hauled the darned heavy sledge along through the snow and across
the salt ice.

Fortunately we were not short of provisions, and we also had enough
paraffin, for we had now reached territory where we had our own
caches. We pressed on for as long as we could, and when we could go no
further, we pitched our tent, which we called the Cheese Cover because
of its smallness and lack of ventilation. Eleven square feet was the extent
of its floor space, and it was scarcely three feet high. It was small, but it
was warm, which to us was the most important thing, and we kept the
Primus burning till its flame was almost suffocated by lack of oxygen
and we had to let a little cold air in to revive it. Outside a storm might
be raging, screaming and howling, and snow lashing at the tent which
would become stiff with ice and heavy and unwieldy. One such storm

lasted six days, during which we were not able to move; and after that we again abandoned all our belongings to the angry gods and set off southwards carrying some food in a bag on our backs, a little paraffin, a rifle and a spade with which to dig ourselves into the snow, if the weather became too bad again.

Thus we groped our way through the darkness, till a brightness came into the sky and we could see where we were treading. The light lasted only a short time, however, and when it had gone and the stars at last were twinkling and sparkling in the black heavens, we still stumbled on through the dark, till we could go no more. Then we found a snow-drift, dug a hole in its side and crawled in, closing the entrance with a plug of snow and leaving the storm and the dark to keep each other company in the bitter night outside.

It was cosy in such a clean little snow den, light and warm — too warm once, for Iver complained after a while that he was almost lying in a pool of water! Not wanting to discuss that all night, I told Iver that he had better lie on the spade, for the wet would not come through that. Iver thought it an excellent idea and got himself settled, while I went to sleep again — but I was roused again a little later by the swearing of a frozen Iver: lying on an iron spade in a temperature of twenty or thirty below had not proved such a good idea. I had not thought of that when I told him to do it!

The days passed, and still we trudged southwards with our few belongings on our backs. We made relatively good speed, for the weather had miraculously turned fine and the ice was not too bad. Then, at last, one day when the light came, we saw land, Shannon Island, the goal that we had been struggling for months to reach, where lay our ship and our companions, in a way our home.

The daylight went and it was night again, cold, black night, with only the stars shining. We set course by a star, found ourselves on land, slipped on stones, fell into holes and up to our waists in snow. But what did it matter? Not a thing! Within an hour our eight months' sledge journey would be over and we home. The moon rose, only a paltry little moon, scarcely a half moon, but it did shed a little light on land and ice, shining like the joy in our hearts: An hour, Iver — in half an hour, Iver — In a quarter of an hour — think, Iver, in a quarter of an hour we will be home again.

We ran across the ice in breathless excitement: Iver, we've won the race with hunger, water and exhaustion. Over there by the black rocks, just under the moon, that's where the winter harbour must be, the ship and the others. Incredible thought — that there should be other people again after eight months of there being just the two of us.

Suddenly I gave a start and halted so abruptly that Iver bumped into me. With a hand that shook I pointed up at the recumbent moon: "Iver, look! Iver, the ship *is* there. Iver, don't you see, the moon's bisected by *Alabama*'s mast?"

He saw what I saw, and we shouted with joy, hallooed and laughed, yodelled and called out.

Were they never going to hear us? We were making enough noise to rouse the dead, yet we heard no glad shouts or barks of welcome, and neither man nor dog came storming to meet us. Iver and I halted, amazed and rather uneasy: what did the silence forebode? The ship was there, but all was as silent as the grave. Where were the others?

I stared fixedly at the mast and discovered that something must be wrong. The mast was in such a queer position and looked remarkably neglected. We still could not see the ship, which was strange, for where the mast was, the ship should be too. It was also extraordinary that we had not been heard by either dogs or men.

Yet the mast was there. We could see it distinctly now, so the ship could not be far away. Perhaps she had been mishandled by the ice. Not that that mattered so much, for we were sure now that the others must be somewhere near the mast. They could not have got away without the ship, so there was no question of our being disappointed of the reunion to which we had been looking forward so tremendously, and that was the most important thing for Iver and me, who had been alone together for nearly eight months.

We walked on across the ice, stumbling among strange objects which we could not identify by the light of a half-moon, and then all at once we were facing something large and black: *Alabama*'s stern? But no, it was not her stern, despite the skylight we could see. Could it be a house? Built on land of *Alabama*'s wreck!

All was oppressively still round us, and everything looked strangely ghostly in the faint moonlight; it was rather sinister. There was not a footprint of dog or man to be seen in the snow, not an empty tin thrown out, none of the innumerable signs of the presence of men and dogs, signs that are inevitable where people are. It was strange, very strange.

But they must be there in the house! We were now close to it, and together we shouted out into the dark, silent night: "Turn out, lads. The wayfarers are back at last."

We listened, but there was not a sound to be heard. Strange! It was as though our glad triumphant shout had encountered something evil and inimical, something unreal in the all but palpable silence.

Then we discovered the door of the house and took a couple of quick strides towards it, but checked in amazement: there was not a footprint to be seen, and the snow reached so high up the door, that it could not have been opened since the autumnal snow began to fall three months before.

The others must have gone. The hut was empty and Iver and I alone in Greenland — east of the sun, west of the moon and in the midst of a white hell.

We said not a word to each other, scarcely even thought; we just kicked the snow away from the door, forced it open and saw — a compact mass of snow grinning at us, instead of the black space we had expected.

Quietly, cowed by disappointment, loneliness and the sinister atmosphere, we set about throwing enough snow out of the hut to let us in; but when we got in, it was only to discover that we could see stars, the moon and some reddish Northern Lights shining through gaps between the planks of the roof. The sail which they had stretched over the roof must have blown away in a storm.

Adversity was an old friend of ours, and in its hard school we had learned to see the good side of any awkward situation, however small. So it was now: "Well, well," said Iver with a sigh, when at last we had dug our way into the hut, "this is a fine mess, but at least it's better than having to lie in another snowdrift tonight."

He was right. Another night in a snowdrift would have been hard to endure. We had also reached our journey's end, and there was no need to trudge on in the morning. Although our home-coming had proved very different from what we had imagined, there were bright spots if you liked to see them, quite bright ones indeed, for as far as we could see part of the provisions appeared to have been salvaged from the ship, so that we ought to have enough for the long winter. That was always something to be glad of.

We crawled into our sleeping bags and fell asleep, and the next day we had other things than our disappointment to think about. There was the roof to cover with the ship's heavy sail, and the hut to be emptied of snow. The nearby food store had to be investigated, and when a faint glow of daylight came at noon, we went out on to the ice to look at what remained of our good ship and try to guess the reason for her loss.

That, however, we were unable to do, for only the stern protruded above the ice. Everything else was hidden beneath a thick layer of ice. We had only wanted to satisfy our understandable curiosity, for the reason for *Alabama*'s loss did not change the situation. The ship was gone, stove in, become a hut on land, and the mast that we had seen, was a flagpole.

But thank God for the hut! It was large and roomy, and provided excellent shelter from the storms that were continually sweeping across land and sea. But that was about all that could be said for it, for its walls were as leaky as the roof had been, and in order to prevent every breath of wind frolicking about the hut, they had nailed sheets of tin on the outside of the walls, which was a splendid idea for keeping the wind out, but disastrous as an attempt at insulation. The thin tin just sucked the heat out of the hut and gave the cold free access. That did not matter so much at night, for we had our sleeping bags and were used to the cold; and by day we managed more or less by keeping the big blow lamp from *Alabama*'s engine going full blast. That managed to get the temperature up to almost 30° C at the level of our heads, but a bucket of water standing on the floor would still freeze in a very short time. To be in anything like a human temperature in the hut, we had to lie on the table; that was not very pleasant, but it was a thing that you could do, if circumstances required it.

The time passed in doing the little jobs that winter allowed, almost all of them indoors. Now and again, when some wandering bear got wind of our winter den and felt impelled to investigate it, we had a hunt. If this happened in the faint daylight, or when the moon was full, it usually resulted in the death of the bear; but if there was no moon, we usually had to leave the bear alone and keep indoors, however much of a shindy it made — even when it bumped against the hut with dull thuds. Such visits were not pleasant, and we were always very careful when an urgent errand sent us out into the cold; for a patient bear might have yielded to its incredible inquisitiveness and lain down in the snow to wait for us to come out.

One night I was awakened by horrified exclamations and violent movements in Iver's bunk: "What is it, Iver, are you ill?"

His answering whisper sent a cold shiver down my back: "Sssh! God help me, but there's a bear in here . . ." And the next moment I heard him throw something at the door and hiss: "Get out, will you!"

We kept both our rifles beside the door, so that we could get them without waste of time, if there should be a bear to go after under normal conditions. We had never envisaged the possibility of having a bear inside the hut.

As quickly as I could, I struck a light and got a candle lit. Iver and I were half out of our bunks, as the light flared up and fell on the whiteness that was the cause of all the commotion. Luckily it was not a bear, but merely the hoar-frosted hindquarters of a musk ox, which was hanging by the door and now lit by a moon-beam that had found its way in through a hole in the roof!

Iver was sick of the sound of the word "bear" by the time we turned out next morning, but when we began going about our day-time occupations in the darkness that we called day, his honour was to some extent rehabilitated, for a bear had paid us a visit during the night. It had scented the quarter of musk ox and made a determined effort to get it, even knocking a hole in the door and causing other damage, but the hut had withstood its attack.

After that we kept one of the rifles where we could reach it from the bunks, and the other by the door, so that bears could come when and as they liked and we would be ready to receive them.

We had a number of foxes living as permanent pensioners in the snow-drifts round the hut; noisy brutes they were, but they enjoyed good living round the door where we threw all our refuse. Now and again other foxes came without invitation, and then there would be a violent fight with much barking and howling, that usually forced us to intervene and try to restore peace with a rifle bullet, a stick or anything handy that could hit hard. Peace was not easy to achieve.

Our work was mostly indoors, and it was a good thing that it was, for the cold was fierce and there were scarcely any intervals between the storms, violent storms at that. We were thus glad to be sheltered as we attended to our little jobs, especially the preparation of food. This was Iver's job, and by degrees he learned to bake bread pretty well and also to cook rice, so that you could almost tell in advance whether the finished product was to be rice or rice-pudding. There is more art to that, than most people think.

One day when we had already been quite a time at the hut, it occurred to us that we ought to do what we had not thought of doing for eight months, which was to wash. We made great preparations: lit the blow-lamp, stoked the stove till it was red-hot and fetched great blocks of ice to melt for water; yet even so there was not a great deal of washing done. We had managed so long without, that we could see no particular reason to go to all that trouble just for the sake of cleanliness. We were by ourselves, so for whom were we washing?

On Christmas Eve, however, we both got a bad attack of homesickness, which we tried to cure with a dose of cleanliness. That did help a little, but Iver was right when he said that it took evil to drive out evil.

Outside a storm was raging, tugging and shaking at the sail nailed to the roof, making it flap so violently that we were continually expecting it to be torn loose and swept away. The storm howled and shrieked round the corners of the hut, rattled the chimney so that it sounded as though a wild animal were caged there. It whistled and screeched, it creaked and crashed, it sounded as though all the devils in Hell had been loosed and had made our solitary hut in the Far North their rendezvous in that dark, wild night. If we peered out cautiously through the door, we could see devils in ghostly white garb whisking round in a senseless dance. For the snow was drifting, sweeping past, whipping up an endless army of strange snow-figures from round the hut, blurred, ghostly shapes, ever changing in wild career and flight, following each other southwards towards destruction.

Outside was not a place to be. It was quite uncanny, all the things you *thought* you could see and hear.

Not that it was so much better inside, where the reeking blow-lamp emitted a long, blue-red tongue of flame that flickered in the draught, as did the candles, making grotesque black shadows.

It was as horrible inside as out, and it was also Christmas Eve. Iver and I looked at each other and did not have as much to talk about as usual, for our thoughts kept following the stormy north wind to milder climes, to those at home who were celebrating Christmas with an empty place at table and an anxious longing in their hearts. That was unhealthy for two lonely men, and we thrust such thoughts aside as far as we could, eating the best that the hut could provide and washing it down with a bottle of beer that we had found outside in the snow.

It was a queer looking bottle of beer, for in freezing the beer had forced the cork out and was protruding from the neck of the bottle, like a bent finger some four inches long. We broke off the finger, thawed the beer in a pan and tried to pretend that it tasted all right. We shared our last glass of whisky to drink to absent friends, and so crawled into our bunks with all our clothes on, for we intended at least to be warm for Christmas.

We did not get much sleep, however, for just as we were at our most woeful, it suddenly occurred to us that after all we had good reason to celebrate, for the sun had now halted in its flight towards the south and was on its way back towards us with light and lovely colours in its train, and with them the promise of summer, a ship and a homecoming.

It really did feel as though that realization had relieved the press of winter. Or did we merely feel that because we had gradually become rested and overcome the everlasting hunger that had tormented us for the best part of six months? At all events our spirits improved from Christmas on, became better and better as the days passed and the patch of lightness in the south crept higher and higher up the sky.

We began to feel a renewal of interest in the future, though not in the immediate future which could only offer us a 200-mile sledge journey north to the skerry where we had left our diaries, and the same distance back again. Four hundred miles in all. It was a darned long way, and we tried to calculate how many steps it would take to cover 400 miles: it was an incredible number. We cursed the diaries which we had abandoned there in a moment of panic, when we thought that we could see death sitting waiting for us by the next headland.

Matters were not improved, when one night I dreamed that I was on the skerry and saw a bear come trotting along the ice and catch the scent of our bundle in the crack in the rock. I had no rifle and could not shoot the bear, which hissed at me and lunged out with a great paw, when I tried to drive it away with shouts and my sheath-knife. So, unable to do anything to stop it, I had to watch the bear dig our bundle of diaries out of the snow, tear and bite at it, split it open with its sharp claws and teeth, and scatter the contents over the snow so that the howling wind could sweep away all that we had struggled so hard to achieve. And I saw our precious diaries fly away on the wind, like small black birds borne on the wings of the storm.

It was a nasty dream and the recollection of it kept cropping up to act as a wet blanket, when we were feeling light-hearted and wanting to sing for joy — not because anything special had happened, but just because it was good to be alive in spite of everything, and because the sun would soon be back again. Nor could we grieve long over a wretched dream that could not have any significance.

CHAPTER XVI

Spring and Summer Hope

Winter's talk — The skerry with the diaries — A dream proves true —
Plans for the future — Iver has a visitor — Difficult pack ice —
Autumn — We give up hope of a ship

New Year's Day and most of January now lay behind us, and the wintry darkness was no longer so oppressive. It was growing lighter every day and already the clouds had acquired a golden sheen, the snow-clad mountains in the north stood out in golden splendour against the dark heavens, and the northern slopes were clad in sharp, white-blue shadow.

We would soon be able to get out again, away from the horrible untidy room in which we had spent the harsh winter months. It would not be long before we could test our strength on a fresh sledge journey. We were young, well-fed, rested and bursting with energy that required an outlet. Our thoughts sped north to the golden mountains, to the skerry where our diaries and journals were, we hoped unharmed by bear or other mishap. Our thoughts also went far to the south to lands where there were other people, men of enterprise and attractive women: "You, Iver, what would you do, if a girl suddenly came walking across the ice towards us?"

Improbable? Yes, but it could have happened. So much that is strange and unexpected does happen, so why not that? Where could she come from? It was not impossible to imagine that somewhere or other a bit to the south of us, a ship had been wintering, a ship with a girl aboard.

Admittedly that was fairly "improbable," but not improbable enough for Iver, whose mind worked on other and more complicated lines than mine, for when he heard that casual suggestion, he, the mechanically minded, at once thought of other possible means of transport than an old-fashioned ship. Before he sailed north in 1909 Iver had seen a Zeppelin over Copenhagen, and he considered it perfectly natural that there might be a Zeppelin flying round in space with a lot of very boring men, but also some pretty women, on board her. And such a Zeppelin could just as well land at Shannon Island as anywhere else, couldn't it?

That was perfectly true, and it opened up fantastic perspectives. Then we began talking about how strange it would be to see women again, elegant, beautiful women, as pure as the flakes of snow that were being borne along by the spring breeze. How chivalrous we would be to those unfortunates, who suddenly dropped down beside us two savages who had not seen a woman for a couple of years. We would do everything to help them, in the most unselfish manner. After all we knew the country and how you got much out of nothing. We would . . . my imagination began to run riot, till it was checked by Iver suddenly saying: "Yes, and then we would have to wash, wouldn't we?" We looked at ourselves in the mirror: grimy, bearded faces and long hair; we looked awful: it was a depressing sight, for we realized that we could not captivate even the most unfastidious woman.

We usually found no lack of topics for conversation and had told each other more about ourselves and aspirations, hopes and dreams than we had ever told anyone before. And we were always able to take some episode from our previous existence, turn it upside down and inside out, and get more out of it than you would have thought possible before. One of our favourite topics was politics. Iver was the reddest of red Social Democrats, a social revolutionary; while I was the scandalized Conservative listening to the unreasonable demands of pink youth with ill-concealed displeasure. We talked and talked, and I do not suppose either of us knew much about what we were discussing. We had neither of us been particularly interested in politics, but it made an excellent topic of conversation. We never quarrelled; just remained steadfastly on our side of the fence and said wise things about what we did not really understand. That, of course, is just what a lot of people do elsewhere in the world, and there was no need to travel to the polar regions for that.

We found a pack of cards and were highly delighted, for that meant that we had something to help pass the dark evenings. Unfortunately we could not remember the rules of any game for two, so we tried to make one up ourselves. That was not very successful. It was not even easy to invent a patience, and I made great efforts to remember one that an advanced Alaskan Eskimo had shown me, a game which he had said was called Idiot's Delight. Iver could not stand Idiot's Delight, so that was no good, and we then tried to work out some other game with a nicer name. That was no good either, so, when we were on the point of squabbling over who knew most about it, I took the pack, walked out with it into the storm and let the wind scatter the fifty-two cards like chaff.

Iver was looking a bit sour when I came in again; but the next day he told me that what I had done was very sensible: that pack of cards might easily have caused us to quarrel, as neither women nor politics had.

All the while we were talking and dreaming of the unattainable, we worked away on a sledge and the equipment we were to use on our 400-mile journey to fetch our diaries and journals. Around noon, if the weather had cleared and the storm for once tired of lashing snow in our faces, we went out and looked towards the south and rejoiced at the growing patch of brightness there, at the glowing blaze that was growing and growing, and one day would flare up into a glorious, life-giving fire that would consume the winter and all its stupid imaginings.

That came about on February 10. The glow in the south suddenly shot arrows of fire across the land at the tired hosts of darkness in the north, striking terror into their hearts and putting them to flight, clothing the land in golden, sparkling splendour, and celebrating its victory over the darkness with a wonderful orgy of colour, which it cast over the whole country, over valley and mountain, ice and land. One of those fiery arrows struck Iver and me on a spur of the mountain, where we had been standing, freezing miserably for the last hour or so, in order not to miss the first sunbeam to be seen in the year 1911.

We stared at that glowing fire, revelling in the thought of the summer that now seemed so near at hand, and of all that would happen to us in that lovely time that was now drawing nearer with giant strides. We greeted the sun with mad shouts of joy that sounded meagre and faint-hearted in all that silence; and high above our heads a black ghost passed, heading for that golden conflagration, a loudly croaking raven, at which we cast jealous looks: if only we could borrow its wings and fly over land and sea to the goal of our dreams. But that sort of thing only happened in the old days, when magic was still made, and not in our prosaic age.

Although we could not borrow the raven's wings and no Zeppelin dropped out of the skies to bring us beauteous maidens, it was nonetheless glorious to see the sun, and when the most painful of the barbs of the cold had been melted by the swift northward course of the sun, we put the traces over our shoulders and began our laborious trudge north. We walked for weeks, three whole weeks, before we reached the skerry. We hauled the sledge all along Koldewey Island and past Danmarks Havn; we gave nods of recognition to headlands and islands, that we had passed the previous autumn on our way to Shannon Island, and to the icebergs that the frost had halted in their voyage to the south, shadowy shapes they had been, scarcely visible in the wintry gloom, but now they were golden and resplendent in the midday sun, lovely, friendly and almost warm-looking, quite different from the prim mileposts we had passed in the black sad days of autumn.

It was lovely and sunny, and we rejoiced in the good progress we were making, as we followed the well-trodden bear tracks along the shore, which often helped us to juicy bear-steaks; yet despite this and our weariness after hauling the sledge for ten or twelve hours through all sorts of snow, in which the going was heavy at the best, the memory of that damned dream was always with us, the dream that had nearly spoilt our peace of mind during the winter.

Countless times we had said to each other: "Supposing the dream were true!" Almost every time we wakened in the night and listened to the sounds of the ice, the almost comprehensible speech of the frost and the wind's chatter, the terrible thought returned: "Suppose that when we get there, we find the dream come true!"

Gradually we drew near the flat white mound that marked our skerry. Beneath that snow lay our diaries and journals, or so we hoped. We were so eager to put an end to the awful doubt the dream had cast into our minds, that we left the sledge standing on the ice and hurried on towards the white hump so as to find out as quickly as possible. But, when we got closer, we halted in amazement: we had not expected so much snow! There was not a dark patch to be seen on the skerry, nor was there a sign of the three or four stones we had built up vertically on edge to act as a cairn beside the diaries.

It was a big skerry, about half a square mile, and about 150 feet high. The whole area was completely covered by a gigantic snow-drift, and somewhere or other beneath all that snow were our diaries.

But where?

Appalled, we stood on the top of the island and surveyed the white expanse. Iver had brought a spade and as he looked at me, I read in his eyes the unuttered question: Where shall I dig?

"Dig?" I said replying to the unspoken query. "Dig where you like. Where you're standing, for example, or six feet away. It amounts to the same thing, for we are not going to find the diaries in all that snow."

Iver took me at my word, thrust the spade into the snow just where he was standing — and gave a loud shout: the first thrust had struck a diary! The next revealed a piece of the cloth in which the diaries had been wrapped. It took only ten spadefuls to unearth all that we had left there on that bitter autumn day, all except one of my diaries, and for that we dug all day without finding more than a few chewed pieces of its leaves.

A bear had been there, just as I had dreamed.

It had been a hungry bear, too, for it had chewed everything that could be chewed. One cartridge had been quite flattened; it was a wonder it had not exploded in the bear's mouth.

It was two happy men who pitched their tent there later that evening, for the loss of my one diary was of no great significance, since that period was still covered by Iver's diary.

Now we would go home, as we could with a reasonably good conscience. We had done what we had undertaken to do, and the

damned bear had not eaten up our results. There was every reason
to rejoice. The sun was shining, the tent was warm and tight, we
made coffee and cooked ourselves a meal, and as we ate and drank we
remembered the bad days. We talked of the journey home, not of the
200 miles back to the hut, that counted for nothing now that we had
the diaries, but of the proper journey home across the seas to Denmark,
to sunshine and summer, green woods and golden fields, to family and
friends, to her, whoever she was, to whom our thoughts went whenever
our minds were not weighed down with other things.

We returned to the hut at Shannon Island, and in the bright light of
high summer its interior looked so dirty, so grim and melancholy and
depressing, that we said goodbye to it as soon as possible, and hoped
never to see it again.

We set off southwards, wading through soggy snow, splashing through
shallow lakes on the ice, and struggling across muddy clay on land,
making for a little hut on the south-east point of Shannon. This was one
of four small huts erected by the American explorer Baldwin, in 1901, and
which he had filled with so much lovely food, that the tale of it was heard
by all who came for a shorter or longer time to the northern coast of East
Greenland in those early days at the beginning of this century.

We were very doubtful whether there really could be so many good
things in the insignificant little hut as rumour said, but we were pleasantly
surprised when eventually we got there. So we settled down on that outer
headland to await the ship that would come in the course of the next
month or so, and take us east to the glories of the ordinary world.

It was a relief to have taken the last step of our long journey and to
have reached its end, so that we could with a good conscience enjoy
ourselves in the hut, which we ransacked and made the most of its store
of provisions. (How I and my companions on the Baldwin–Ziegler
Expedition would have enjoyed them ten years before, when we tried
to reach the Pole from Kaiser Franz Josephs Land! The intention, then,
had been that we should return via the east coast of Greenland, but we
never got as far.)

We settled ourselves into the hut, where we found a letter from our companions, telling us that they had left the winter harbour at the end of August in a little Norwegian sealer. They had waited for us as long as they possibly could, and they had even got the sealer to sail a little way north to look for us. But we were then right up at Lamberts Land! And so they had sailed for home, as they had been ordered to do; and there we now were, waiting for a ship.

It was not long before the evil spirits of East Greenland dropped a little gall into our cup, sending us a cold summer, as a result of which mist lay thick and impenetrable over the pack ice, hiding the sun from us, often for days on end. Nor were the results of our hunting as good as we had hoped, chiefly because we were reluctant to go far from the hut, since it was always possible that a ship might be lying off somewhere out in the mist, and so might reach land at any moment. We did, in fact, often hear noises like those from a ship, coming from the clammy world of the mist, so naturally we kept near the place to which the ship would come. The ship was sure not to be able to wait for us, for the winds and currents were keeping the ice in too much motion for her to be able to do that. Thus things were not all that they might have been, and, to be candid, our stay on that outer headland was not what we had anticipated.

Now and again, in fact quite often, we saw things on the ice that imagination and refraction transformed into mast and ship, to people hastening across the great ice floes. But on each occasion we were disappointed. In the beginning we talked of the ineffable joy it would be, when the ship came at last; but as time went on, as June turned into July and then all too quickly August was there, we spoke less and less of the joy it would be to see the ship, preferred not to speak of the ship at all, so as not to start an avalanche of dreary thoughts about the future and what our fate would be, if the ship did not come after all.

However, we found that we forgot the tardy ship when we were occupied with work or busy planning what we could do with all the years of the future; for when you are only thirty you feel yourself entitled to a good many. We had many plans, but there was one in particular that soon won preference over all the others and which we found especially attractive, that of repopulating the empty coast of North-East Greenland.

The origin of the plan was a very obvious one, for wherever we went on Shannon, we found quite numerous traces of former habitation. We had also seen similar traces in many places farther north, huts fallen into ruin, stone traps for bear and fox; so, when we felt lonely and abandoned, we derived a sort of encouragement from talking about the paradise the coast could have been, if there had been Eskimos to be met — as in the olden days — beyond the point where there were the ruins of a dozen houses.

But could Eskimos live where we with our rifles had all but perished from starvation? There was no disguising the fact that we had not bagged anything worth mentioning, certainly not enough to live off. But we had seen both bear and seal, and a certain amount of smaller game, and we were convinced that Eskimos who were familiar with the country, and who lived there more or less permanently and thus would know the best hunting areas and times, would be able to get enough on land and sea to keep themselves going, and probably much more.

Once we started talking about what there had been in the past, it was inevitable that we should begin discussing the possibility of repopulating the coast, of moving Eskimos from the over-populated areas of West Greenland to East Greenland, where in our opinion there was a livelihood to be had for many. In imagination Iver and I could see satisfied Eskimos living here and there up and down the coast, and before long we were saying happily that in a few years time, perhaps, you would be able to see a women's boat rounding the south-east point of Shannon, followed by four or five men in kayaks. We looked at our maps and tried to decide where would be the best points for Eskimo immigration.

They could certainly exist on Shannon, the island where we were waiting for our ship, and at Danmarks Havn, and up the big fjords with their calm, shiny water. The many ruins of houses, both where we were and elsewhere, had a convincing tale to tell. But Shannon

Island was perhaps too far north, and the distance too great to the only inhabited place in East Greenland, Angmagssalik; so we compromised and agreed that Scoresby Sound was perhaps the most suitable place for a new colony. Hunting was good there, as I knew from the Amdrup Expedition, and in the old days many Eskimos had lived on that great fjord, the biggest in the world.

We found it a splendid plan with which to occupy our minds during those hours, when the longing to see someone other than the one miserable wretch we were always looking at, was especially strong. Suppose the plan had already been put into effect and we might expect at any moment to see a women's boat come paddling through the floes filled with happy, laughing Eskimo women. And suppose that they, nodding and smiling enticingly, were to go up the mountain-side and summon the two fools who in their masculine arrogance had believed that they could get along by themselves in that harsh land, but now realized how hopeless that was.

These Eskimos with whom in imagination we gradually peopled the coast soon seemed anything but stupid fantasies. They were so real to us that we often forgot that they were mere creations of imagination, conceived by our crushing sense of loneliness. But at least they gave us something to think about while we waited longingly for the mist to lift, so that we could see the ship that must be lying off from the hut, or at least making its way through the pack ice towards us. We went up the mountain-side whenever the mist lifted and scanned the wilderness of dense ice, that extended as far out to sea as our gaze would reach. It would not be easy for any ship to get through that.

Then one day something quite sensational and most unexpected happened: Iver received a visitor.

He had gone out with his rifle and returned sooner than I had expected. He looked rather bewildered and went and sat down quietly on a stone. That was so unlike him, for he was usually most cheerful, that I asked what had happened.

I was prepared for any answer except the one I was given. Iver looked at me, astonishment in his eyes, and said quietly: "I've seen my grandfather; he was sitting on a stone up there" — and Iver pointed up towards the high ground. "He must be dead."

A cold shiver ran down my back, and I looked sharply at Iver. He appeared perfectly normal, though there was an expression in his eyes I had not seen before — and I thought I knew him pretty well. That he should have said that about his grandfather came as a surprise, and I said as much, and tried to dismiss the whole thing as nonsense; but Iver insisted: "He was sitting up there on a stone. He had on the red cap that he always wears, and I recognized his suit. It was grandfather, that's quite certain. He must be dead now," Iver said quietly, "he and I were such good friends."

Iver and I walked together to the stone where his grandfather had been sitting, but he was no longer there. Iver, however, still insisted that he had seen him. One day, more than forty years afterwards, I asked Iver if he really had believed that he had seen him, and he nodded: "I saw him, Mikki. It was grandfather. And when I came home, I learned that he had died just at that time."

It sounds very odd, but there is yet another example: one day shortly after our return home, my mother asked me what had happened to me on a certain day, the date of which was written on a piece of paper she showed me. It was a date I knew; I remembered it at once, for on that day my life had been in grave danger. I do not know whether I had thought of mother particularly intently, but it is possible. You think so much and so swiftly, when you suddenly discover that there is only a second or two's sand left in your hour-glass.

What is one to believe? You do not need to be hysterical or occupied with *-isms* to find yourself thinking on occasion, that there is more between Heaven and earth than the exact sciences can explain or will admit. I find myself thinking, too, of that distant day in Calcutta roads, when an Indian foretold me a future in a land so white and desolate that he had never imagined anything like it. Up to 1912 that prophecy had been kept pretty well, and later it became truer than ever.

We did not have much time, however, to wonder about weird

happenings, nor much desire; for we suddenly realized that the days had sped whilst we waited for the ship. Most of August had already flown, like the migrant birds that were winging their way south, passing over our heads as we sat by the flagstaff staring out across the ice-covered sea. They quacked and jabbered as they passed overhead on their way south, and we gazed viciously at the flag that in happier days we had hung in a bag by the flagpole, so that it should be ready to hoist without loss of time, when we saw a ship out in the ice.

But the ship never arrived. Instead of it came dark nights with stars, colourful Northern Lights and cold so fierce that the ground became as hard as armour-plate in the course of one night, and every puddle on land or pool on sea was made shiny with new ice. Gone was the blue bells' soft ringing in summer breezes; the purple flowers of our rose-bay had been powdered white. All vegetation had stiffened in the cold, and the delicate stems that had withstood so many stormy gusts during the heat of summer, became brittle and snapped with small reports, when the harsh wind of autumn blew across the land.

The mountain tops round us became powdered with the finest of new-fallen snow, and glistened whitely as they towered towards the pallid sky, their shadows blue-black. Not infrequently the outlines of the mountains were veiled, or became blurred and indistinct, and then we knew that dirty weather was brewing up there in the heights. Storm-clouds came tumbling down the steep mountain-sides. Autumn was upon us and winter near. Only fools could expect a ship so late; yet we still waited, and our eyes gazed longingly at the migrating birds that chattered and quacked so expectantly and joyfully, as they flew past towards the light and warmth of the south.

The two of us were left there in that desolate land, feeling more and more forlorn. Soon there would only be stragglers from the migrating flocks left, and the country's own animals: long-haired musk oxen, agile foxes, lurking wolves and snuffing bear. And we two!

The migration ceased. We no longer heard the sharp clangour of the terns or the hoarse cackle of the gulls, only the ominous screech of the ravens. On land we neither saw nor heard the nimble little birds that had delighted us so greatly in the summer. The seals no longer sunned themselves on land or ice, but warmed themselves in the cold black water. The fox cubs and leverets had grown up and were having to fend for themselves; winter was very near, a long, dark winter, interminably long and dark.

CHAPTER XVII

The Third Winter

The ship never came — Plans to get to Angmagssalik
by ourselves — The dinghy is wrecked on land — Bass Rock —
A grim cross — Two ships looked for us — A dual existence —
Would we have, or would we not? — Pensioners and a trap's victims

We had to face up to realities and, grim though the outlook might be, get ready to spend a third winter in Greenland. During this we had also to make preparation for the following summer, when we intended to try to get away by ourselves, instead of sitting with our hands in our laps waiting for a ship.

While we had been waiting and still hoping, we had sometimes talked, first as a joke and then seriously, of bringing the dinghy from the winter harbour down to this south-eastern point of Shannon, so that as soon as there was open water in the spring, we could sail south to Angmagssalik, where we would find people.

It was 1,300 miles to Angmagssalik which was a very long way, but there was nothing discouraging in that, for the current always flows south along the coast of East Greenland, and that at quite a good rate. It would make things considerably easier, if we could get the dinghy up on to some large ice floe, which would drift day and night and carry us with it southwards to our distant goal.

In the summer we would certainly be able to hasten our progress by putting the dinghy into the water and either rowing or sailing, if the wind were favourable. The thing was quite possible, given a little luck; and if we did not manage it, well, hard work and reasonable hopes of reaching people were always better than sitting and just waiting, waiting, without being able to do anything to avert the fate that awaited us.

So we left the hut, where we had met with such disappointments, and walked back home to — yes, where was our home? Everywhere, I suppose, where we had a tiny hut, a den where, like other of the country's animals, we could seek shelter from the cold and the storms that whipped like scourges.

In this case our home was our old winter quarters, and with our gear in a bundle on our backs we trudged across ice and land to get the dinghy that in the following spring was to carry us south — to people!

We felt much better, once we had definitely given up all hope of the ship coming that year. Iver was a magnificent companion, and if ever two people got on well together, it was he and I. We knew each other's innermost being and thoughts; we knew what reaction we could expect from the other in all circumstances, and we were both convinced that we could get through another winter, as long as we were together — and in good health. But, in talking of this as we had many times, we had also agreed that if one of us went, the other would not be able to live: two together could manage, but one alone? Never!

As usual when we were toiling at something together, Iver found a song to suit the occasion, and while we trudged north we bawled out into the cold and darkness: "So here we sit for the third year running, third year running, third year running" — and then a bit more which I have forgotten, and tralala. We thought it sounded quite lovely, and somehow or other it relieved our minds after the disappointment.

A successful musk oxen hunt that provided us with meat enough to last for a long time further improved our spirits. It was horribly cold at night lying on the frozen ground wondering whether the daylight would not soon be putting the stars to flight; but that was only for a few days, and then we came to the hut which we had hoped never to see again.

The walls were covered with sparkling hoar-frost, and it smelled sour and mouldy inside. It was a dismal, depressing dwelling, but tucked away in it were a number of things that we would need during the coming winter and on our journey south in the spring. And there was work to do! We had a sledge to build, a sledge strong enough to

carry the dinghy; and then the meat of the musk oxen we had shot had
to be cut, dried and frozen. In fact, there were hundreds of little things
to be done, quite enough to keep us busy in that hut on the north-east
point of Shannon Island, which was our temporary home.

Storms fell upon us, as they do every autumn. Snow swept across
the land, while the ice was cleft by long frost-fissures and sighed and
moaned. It became darker and darker every day, and instinct sent the
animals to their dens under big stones, or they sought warmth beneath
the thick cover of the snow. We knew it all and accepted it patiently,
sewing garments, making the sledge, overhauling the dinghy — and
what a hard struggle it was getting the heavy thing on to the sledge
and lashed down! It was quite out of the question that we could haul
the sledge without help, so we stepped the dinghy's mast, made a sail
and hoped that the wind would help us take our heavy, but precious
burden south.

All our preparations took time. The days of storm and enforced
inactivity were sometimes long, for we had nothing to read but two
newspapers, dated prior to our departure from Copenhagen. These
precious things had been used as mere wrapping, but of course there
was plenty of reading matter to be had in Copenhagen. We, however,
were very glad of our two newspapers; they were read, discussed and
construed in every possible way. It was really quite amusing and gave
us a lot of fresh topics of conversation, and we were able to invent long
stories from the advertisements, especially the marriage ones.

New topics were most welcome, for we knew each other's opinion
on everything under the sun and could scarcely start talking about
anything without knowing exactly what the other would have to say
about it. We were on the point of growing tired of each other's voices,
and it was becoming difficult to raise a smile at jokes and sayings we
had heard hundreds of times before.

The first week or two after we had given up hope of the ship were
difficult to get through, there being too crass a difference between the
life we were living and would have to live for the best part of another
year, and that we had hoped to be able to lead at home in Denmark. But

dreary as life was in the hut, that never affected our friendship: hasty words that we would have regretted afterwards might spring to our lips at times, but they never passed them. Such words had to be held back, so that we should not later have to rue the hasty stupid things we had said.

In the middle of October we left the hut at the north-east point of Shannon Island. We hoisted sail on the dinghy that was lashed fast to a stout sledge, and we also had a sail on another sledge that carried all our gear, and with this little squadron we set off south before a fresh north wind. The wind seared and stung where it found its way in through the holes in our clothing, but as it was also driving our heavy sledges along nicely, we just had to freeze with a good grace. For a couple of days all went reasonably well, and we had covered more than half the distance, when in a squall I drove the sledge with the dinghy into a huge snowdrift, and there it stuck. The mast blew overboard, the sail followed the driving snow and vanished into the darkness, while snow kept falling by the cart-load, swirling round us so that we could not see. When we eventually got a grasp of the situation, it was quite clear that we must abandon the dinghy; it was hopelessly stuck and was being rapidly buried under a mountain of snow.

That was the end of our hopes of being able to sail or drift on an ice floe down to Angmagssalik in the spring, and it was two very depressed men who somehow or other hauled the other heavy sledge to the hut at the south-east point of Shannon.

We had by degrees become fed-up with Shannon, which seemed to have a hoodoo on it. Everything we had undertaken there had turned out quite differently to what we had intended. The disappointments had been many and the joys few, so we decided to get away from it and take advantage of the first good weather and fair wind to "sail" the sledge across to Bass Rock, where there were two more of Baldwin's huts, the contents of which I was entitled to use.

It was not far across the sea to Bass Rock, just over thirty miles, and as we had the wind with us we sped quickly across the ice. To leeward, only a few hundred yards away, was a seemingly open sea lashed into foam by a stiff north wind. The waves washed up over the edge of the ice, spray came hurtling through the air and rattled against the sail, sledge and us, hurting like the stab of a knife when it struck our unprotected faces. Large pieces were continually breaking off the edge of the ice and drifting out to sea, bringing the open water nearer and nearer towards where we were. It looked pretty dangerous. But we reached Bass Rock, and there we stopped in amazement when we saw what was on the shore: a tall pole to the top of which was nailed a horizontal board, a cross in the wilderness where before there had been nothing! Iver and I looked at each other in bewilderment: there must have been people there even after our companions had left. And was that cross, perhaps, raised in memory of us?

That we never discovered. There was no explanation of the cross to be found on Bass Rock, nor did I ever find out anything about it later. The cross was there, but no one would admit to having erected it.

To our infinite surprise and dismay there were other, quite unmistakable signs that people had been on Bass Rock, while we were on Shannon keeping watch for a ship. This was all too obvious from two messages we found nailed to the wall in the hut: one was from a sealer, which had helped itself liberally to the provisions in the hut and in return intended to make an attempt to reach Shannon and, if possible, find us. The other was from a Norwegian steam yacht, *Laura*, which had brought a party of Austrian counts and countesses up to East Greenland to give them a thrill.

Was it these aristocratic tourists who had set up the cross?

Laura, of course, had also tried to reach Shannon Island in order to discover what had happened to us; but ice had prevented her getting more than halfway, and so her counts and countesses had missed the thrill they would undoubtedly have got from visiting our summer camp. Not that we were fit to be presented to noble ladies of the Austrian aristocracy, but we did not think of that until later, when we had got over the worst of the disappointment at a ship having been less than fifteen miles from us, and we were back in the routine of every day. At first we were quite numbed by the news, and thought ruefully of what those few miles had meant for us and also for our friends. If we could have got across the previous summer, as we had tried, we would have been on the shore to receive the *Laura* with her counts and countesses, and would thus have saved ourselves six months' anxiety and privation. It was bad enough for us, but that two ships had looked for us and had to turn back with nothing accomplished, must have been a hard blow to our families.

It must indeed be hard for parents to have queer sons, who spend their lives in weird places where life and death go almost hand in hand; but it can also be unpleasant for the sons, when they imagine their parents' grief and worry through not knowing what has happened: knowledge of death deals a hard blow, but it can be overcome gradually; while the nagging torment of uncertainty never stops.

It was this torture of uncertainty our parents now had to bear for another whole year. We felt with them and for them, and we cursed the evil fate that had arranged matters so wretchedly for us, and for all those who thought of us. We were both silent and reserved after we had read the two messages from *Laura* and the sealer, and it must have been the first occasion in our long time together, that neither Iver nor I felt urged to let the other know the thoughts that were preying on our minds: dispirited and depressed, we crawled into our sleeping bags to seek forgetfulness in sleep.

Life has to be lived, however hard it may seem, and in a day or two we had recovered ourselves and uprooted the horrible cross on the beach, so that the sight of it should not arouse our dormant despondency each time we looked that way.

Those were dangerous thoughts we struggled with, and we both realized that the quicker we got them under control the better for us. After all, we could not relieve our parents' sorrow.

Thus we combated our thoughts as best we could and gradually life returned more or less to normal; yet despondency cut deeper and deeper into our minds and became like an open sore that ached each time our thoughts sped southwards.

However, things became better and better by degrees, and even though the sun had long since gone into hibernation, there was still enough light in the sky for us to be able to hunt hares and ptarmigan, and now and again bear. We spent as much time as possible out of doors, where there were twinkling, starry heavens high above us, and away in the distance a wall hung with the draperies of the Northern Lights. The hut was too cramped for us, when our thoughts were sad.

Not much happened in the dark days of autumn and winter, not enough to enable us to have an ordinary conversation about the day's happenings, and thus we had to have recourse to artificial topics to keep the spectre of silence away.

We discussed politics, as we had the previous winter, but from opposite platforms, as though I had convinced Iver that the Conservative policy was better than the one he had been advocating, while I had had to accept his views as a confirmed Socialist; that was the only way we could get a discussion going. It worked quite well — and we were always able to taunt the other good-naturedly by talking back at him some of the nonsense he had advanced before as the height of political wisdom.

Those silly discussions were apt to come to a halt for lack of fuel, and when that happened we took to walking round and round the stove in our little octagonal hut, our heads buzzing with thoughts, while we wrestled with the hideous question: were we to spend a fourth winter there? We could no longer be sure of anything; we could believe nothing, just hope that something would happen.

Fortunately we had another equally silly topic of conversation to fall back on, and that was our dreams, which either came to us naturally or were induced by the simple expedient of eating porridge at night. That was Iver's suggestion, for he had been told that it was an infallable way of dreaming, and thus porridge became for us a sort of gateway to the wide world.

In that third winter, when we had long since threshed out every subject we could think of, we clung to dreams as a topic of conversation, so much so that to all intents and purposes we lived two sorts of life: one by day when nothing special happened, and one at night when we could roam far and wide on the wings of dreams and experience the most glorious adventures.

We went so far in our efforts to regard our dream game as reality that we never asked each other: "What did you dream last night?" But, far more concretely: "Where were you last night?" And so, while we ate our morning porridge, made with mouldy oatmeal, and drank coffee that seemed to have been in too close contact with both carbolic and paraffin, we told each other of our lovely experiences of the night which we had spent in sunshine and warmth, in town or country, but among other people, both men and women, and related what had befallen us in their gay company.

Those dreams could open up unsuspected perspectives and provide things to talk about for a long time, or matter for quite sensible discussions. Iver often visited his ancestral farm, and quite often the first thing he said to me in the morning would be: "I was at Uncle Søren's again last night, and —"

That would set us off, and we might spend hours talking of agriculture and all that we in our wisdom thought touched upon it. It was a good thing we did not have a tape recorder in the hut, for I am sure our cheeks would have blushed in shame if, later in life, we had ever heard what we had expounded to each other then as the height of wisdom. Such horrors are happily soon forgotten, but it still happens that when we meet, a jocular look will come into Iver's eye and he will say: "Do you remember, you said . . ." and then he produces one of my more monstrous pronouncements from those days, and I shudder.

It was a dismal existence for us two lonely men, especially when the polar night was all round us with its almost palpable darkness, which there was nothing but the glow of the sparkling stars to mitigate. It was a great day for us when the moon hung large and round in the black sky and lit up the snow, so that shadows emerged on the white landscape and the ice crystals gleamed and glistened — though not so gaily as in the glow of the spring sunshine.

Then was the time for us to leave our small hut and take a walk across country with a rifle over our shoulder, for we might always meet a bear, a musk ox or at worst a miserable hare. It was a splendid feeling being able to roam about, and when we returned to the hut after some such lengthy wander in the moonlight, we often found that something we had experienced on it had awakened memories of our long sledge journey which now seemed quite a thing of the past, and we often felt an urge to discuss whether it would have been better to have done this or that instead of what we had done.

Ever since then, each time we have dwelt on the last few days of our hunger march, one great question has always cropped up: If the other had died, would we, or would we not, have attempted to save our life by eating him? We are not sure of the answer, but what we do know is that the idea occurred to us both, when the onslaught of hunger was at its worst and we saw how difficult it was for the other to keep going and doubted whether he would do so long enough to reach Danmarks Havn and the food that would save us.

Iver was a bit more definite in his ideas than I, for he maintained that he could not have touched me, unless he had first removed my hands, at least the fingers.

"Why on earth?" I asked in amazement, the first time he told me that.

Quietly, Iver replied: "I don't like thinking of it or talking about it. But it seems to me that hands distinguish humans from animals. It is with their hands that people can do all the things animals cannot do. To me our humanness lies in our hands."

I had never thought of that, but there could be something in it. Having reached the point of discussing what we would or would not have done, when we were all but desperate with hunger and preferred not to carry the rifle that could give death and rest, we usually tried to find a less macabre topic of conversation as quickly as we could. The question, however, has remained at the back of our minds all these years, and just the other day I put it to Iver once again. He gave me the same answer.

It was not always the frivolous we discussed in our little hut that looked so tiny where it stood under the steep high mountain that almost leaned over it. Everything that could bring a little variety to the uniformity of the long dark days was fervently welcomed, or almost everything. But even toothache, if not welcome, at least was effective in breaking the monotony of our days. I remember one bout I had. It began in midwinter and was made no better when the unhappy thought came to me that it could perhaps continue until I got home and could have the tooth drawn. That set me tormenting myself by reckoning out the awful sum: eight months is two hundred and forty days, and that is . . . But why go on, as I did, reckoning out how many hours, minutes and seconds there were in eight months, and imagining myself having toothache for each one of those innumerable seconds. It was awful and became even worse when Iver, in all innocence, told me that in the remote rural districts, when it was a long way to the nearest dentist, they relieved toothache by pouring schnapps on the tooth. We had no schnapps, but we did have a little hospital spirit, and we thought that that ought to have the same effect. And so I took a glass of spirit to get rid of my toothache.

I never want to go through anything like it again. I stamped round the hut uttering loud bellows of pain that quite drowned poor unhappy Iver's excuses, as he ran round after me assuring me that he really had thought that it would help and that he had wished me no harm. I knew that, of course, but it was awful while it lasted, and then to my amazement the cure worked.

We hunted as often as possible for the sake of having fresh food, and so our joy was great when one day in the twilight of noon we discovered hare tracks in the snow. It was too dark to follow them up, or to aim with any accuracy, so instead we set up a trap and hoped that we might entice the hare into it by strewing mouldy oatmeal up to the mouth and putting a large heap of it inside behind the drop.

It was most exciting, and for the first couple of days we took it in turn to keep watch at night, so as to be able to kill the hare at once, if it went into the trap. It was a long time in obliging, or else it did not like mouldy oatmeal; but when the snow grew deeper and the hare more hungry, it was tempted, and great was our joy when we were aroused by a tremendous commotion coming from the trap, in which we found a poor hare shivering with fright.

It looked at us with such frightened eyes that our hearts began to melt and we talked of letting it out, for we were aware of a certain likeness between the hare in the box and ourselves in the immense space that we could not get out of.

Christmas was near, however, and the thought of roast hare for Christmas overpowered our nobler feelings, and the hare died. A couple of days later we almost fell over its mate in the snow and killed that too. Our Christmas fare was thus assured, and we sat in the hut longing for the day when the sun would have gone so far south, that it would have to start making its way back towards the north. Strange as it may seem, we also longed to hear the wind howling round our hut's eight corners, whistling in the chimney and hurling hard frozen crust-snow at our little window.

That December was uncannily still. Now and again we heard wind blustering on the mountain, or it would come and screech round the house and whistle in the chimney, but it only did so for an instant; the next moment the gust would have blown out to sea and have gone, leaving everything as unreally still and silent as before, so silent that we felt an urge to shout and make a noise, to try and awaken echoes in that numbing, oppressive stillness. The silence was broken at times, however, when the pressure of distant storms thrust the pack ice against the land and crushed it with dull roars, rumbles, crashes and splinterings, and that gave us a welcome feeling that the world had not come to a standstill after all, but that there was life and mighty forces moving round us.

Then Christmas came, our third in that part of the world and the second we had spent alone. I had been looking forward to it with considerable apprehension, for that is a time when emotions that are not good for lonely men can so easily gain the upper hand.

Iver was kept busy cooking the hares. We were to have them both, for we were not economizing on anything at Christmas. He was also cooking what he hoped would turn into the traditional Danish rice-pudding, though it could just as easily turn into gruel, that not being easy to determine beforehand. I was no good at cooking, so I had made myself responsible for cleaning the hut. There was not much of that to be done, for the broom had grown quite bald with age and we could not use much water, that being a commodity it cost too much of our precious fuel to produce, and anyway water was no use on the floor, for any spilt there instantly turned to ice. So we left the floor alone, rolled up our sleeping bags, lit our last candle and realized with a sense of satisfaction that, as we had not had any soap for the last two or three months, we need not be ashamed of our unwashed faces and hands on that solemn occasion.

Despite roast hare and the other good things we had, things the Americans had brought there ten years before and which time, mould and acquisitive sealers had spared, our Christmas was as dreary as we had anticipated, and when it drew near the time when we could decently go to bed, one of us went out stealthily into the cold and shut the door of the hare-trap. The chances of getting a hare in the trap were not great, but it was not impossible, and that night we did wish not to hurt or harm any living creature. Even a bear could have come in safety to our door.

No bear came, however, so we earned no haloes. It was a sad and sorrowful Christmas in every respect, and the only joy Iver and I could extract from it, was the thought that now at last the sun was on its way north again. Then we each ate a large helping of porridge and hoped that we might have a merry Christmas in our dreams.

CHAPTER XVIII

The Last Six Months

The products of lonely men's imaginations — The sun returns for the third
time — Daily life in our winter hut — Dear pensioners — Foxes as
messengers — We attempt a sledge journey — Our strength fails us

Once the winter solstice lay behind us and lighter days were in the offing, we began to take more pleasure in life. One day Iver unearthed a hitherto hidden treasure from his private hoard, a collection of some twenty postcards which he spread out on the box that served as our table, asking me if I did not think them lovely. They were. Some were postcards of Copenhagen and these showed such swarms of people that we, who for two years had seen no one but each other, became quite giddy at the sight and wondered if there really still were places in the world where people swarmed like that.

There were also coloured pictures of the country scene with thatched farmhouses, golden fields, brown cows and all the rest of it. One of the cards depicted a large tree in the middle of a green pasture and a girl enjoying the summer in its shade. It was a pretty picture: the grass was so green we almost doubted it could be true, and the sky so blue that it simply cried out: This is summer in Denmark! And the girl was dressed in bright red: lovely, the loveliest of Nature's products.

We nailed that postcard to the wall of the hut, so that the green grass and the girl in red could warm our hearts, when our existence up there in the ice and snow and solitude seemed too awful.

The best of the postcards was one Iver had had from a "cousin," who was attending a school for domestic economy. It too was a summer scene, and the atmosphere of summer simply welled out of it in the guise of the many girls in summery dresses photographed in front of the school building, pretty girls, lovely girls with smiling eyes and mouths.

We looked at that photograph many times, especially when we were down in the dumps. We sought comfort from those happy-looking girls, and we discussed them and tried to discover their characters from the cleanness of their faces, the neatness of their dresses and the straightness of their limbs. Our two dirty, long-haired, bearded heads almost touched as they bent over it, while we, a magnifying glass before our eyes and a smoky paraffin lamp pulled as close as possible, scrutinized all that feminine grace and beauty, which brightened our little hut by the shore of the polar sea.

We agreed that we would not touch the girls on the postcards with our fingers, for our hands were not very clean, and we were afraid that some of the dirt might come off and blur the girls' beautiful features. But as we were to talk with the girls, discuss them and try to discover their good and bad characteristics, they each had to have a name, so that we should know of whom we were speaking. So we named them: there was a Miss Steadfast, a pretty girl in a white dress and a free and easy attitude; Miss Affectation, who leaned against a fence doing all she could to look alluring. There was a Miss Long, a Miss Short, a Miss Sulky, and Iver's special flame, little Miss Sunbeam, who looked so young, so happy and smiling, that it warmed Iver's all but icy heart.

We invented a story about each of these selected girls, and we promised each other that when we got home we would pay the school a visit, see the girls, and find out whether the fine characters we had given them corresponded to reality. I was especially interested in Miss Steadfast and Iver in Miss Sunbeam.

It was indeed a wonderful postcard, and we put it carefully away after each time of feasting our eyes upon it. It gave us matter for many conversations — and food for strange thoughts in hours of loneliness.

The dark period of that third winter was a hard time. To me it seemed darker and more difficult to bear than those that had preceded it. We again began thinking of going with the drifting ice south to Angmagssalik, but for that we must have a boat to take us into the land when we got there, and our boat lay buried beneath a snowdrift on Shannon Island. Perhaps, though, we might be able to salvage the dinghy, when the sun returned and its blazing light had driven the darkness from the land and its warmth made it possible for us to work outdoors.

Yes, the sun! How we longed for it. On clear days we never failed to go outside the hut, and preferably on top, to gaze at the brightness in the south that day by day crept higher into the sky, flushing beneath the caress of the distant sun. The life-giving blaze would soon flare up over the southern horizon, and already the snow on the southern slopes of the mountains was tinged a delicate pink, while all that faced north remained cold, blue-white and forbidding.

The sun would soon be back, and so we had to decide what we could do to get away by our own resources. Even though we still thought ourselves pretty stout fellows, who could stand up to most things, there were various signs showing that the darkness, cold, solitude and unsuitable diet had affected us. Our joints creaked more than was good, our gums were perhaps a little redder than they should have been, and our teeth no longer felt part and parcel of our jaws. And I had something that could not be right: a large swelling on one side of my neck.

Was scurvy going to attack us again?

We had to try to discover what we were still worth, so we set about preparing for a small sledge journey, that would enable us to test our strength and see what possibility there was of our getting away on our own. We began patching up our equipment and overhauling what we called clothes, only to find that there was little of the latter left, but the name. But there was a certain amount of patching we were able to do, and we were also able to make some new things out of untanned bearskin, which is strong and as stiff as tinplate. And we also had some sailcloth, No. oo, which is the heaviest made. In the big sailing ships it used to stand up to hurricanes, so we felt that it ought to make good trousers for Iver. I cut out some pieces and though Iver looked suspiciously at them, I insisted that they would make warm, strong trousers for him. I secured them with a sailmaker's palm and needle, a good seaman's job, though not pretty to look at. The resemblance to trousers was not as great as it perhaps might have been, but at least there were two legs. Iver put the garment on to please me, and then asked, appalled, whether I really intended him to wear it. I did indeed, for those he had been wearing had been ripped up to provide a pattern. The new trousers were good enough, though they might not give as much freedom of movement as they should have. That, however, was easily remedied: it was merely that they were a little too tight in the crutch. Iver lay on his stomach across a packing case and I made him straddle his legs wide, while I took a sharp knife and made a slit where the tightness was. I sewed a piece of canvas in and there were the trousers, as good as we could make them. They were not pretty and as stiff as the very devil, but they wore — they would have lasted a hundred years!

We had no lack of work that winter, for there is plenty to do when there are only two to do the work, plus all the odd jobs that otherwise you do not need to waste time on. We would be pretty well done when evening came and the day's bear's meat steak, or bear stew, was eaten and washed down with coffee tasting of carbolic and paraffin, a taste to which it is even possible to get used, so great is man's adaptability.

After coffee we liked to smoke a cigarette or pipe, while we discussed the day's events or what we would do in the morning. Whilst we smoked and talked, we coughed appallingly, for our tobacco was usually dried tea-leaves and our cigarettes were made of bits of old newspaper, which neither improved the taste nor lessened the quantity of smoke, so that the little hut filled with suffocating fumes, especially on calm days. If there was the least wind blowing, the innumerable draughts would drive the foul air out through the many leaks in the walls of the hut. Otherwise we might have asphyxiated ourselves.

About midwinter we acquired a pet in the shape of a fox that hunger had turned vegetarian, so that it had let itself be enticed into the hare-trap with its heap of musty oatmeal. How pretty and brave it was, when we carried the trap in triumph into the hut, while the fox looked at us with darting, inquisitive and fearless eyes.

It was pretty wild the first few days after we had got it out of the box and tethered it in the hut, but it soon overcame the trembling anxiety of the wild creature and became quite tame. We got a lot of pleasure out of our lively little pet, which shortened many an hour for us, and we were really sorry when, one day, it seized an irresistible chance to dive out of the door and vanished into the white distance, dressed in dirty grey fur as a memento of its short stay in civilization.

When we spoke of our pet, which later came to play a remarkable role in our hermitic existence and gave rise to the strangest hopes and expectations, we called it "Fie," in sour recognition of the fact that it had been very far from house-trained. But then perhaps we were not the right people to have taught it manners.

When we returned to Bass Rock after a small sledge journey we made in the spring, we were met by a fox that halted, glanced up at us with sparkling, almost understanding eyes, and then ran ahead of us to the hut, where it had obviously been living while we were away.

That fox was so tame and trusting that, to our joy, it followed us into the hut almost without hesitation. After a few days' petting it followed us like a dog when we went out, and if it went off by itself to attend to its own affairs, it never went so far that it did not come running back at once when we called and it heard its name: Prut.

One day I saw fox's tracks in the incredibly white snow and naturally assumed that Prut had been out as usual, so I thought no more about it, till I came to some fine, new-fallen snow and there saw a distinct groove running parallel with the tracks. I was almost as surprised as Robinson Crusoe when he first saw Friday's footprints, and I stood quite still so as not to lose the tracks again. I called to Iver and showed him the track: "What is it, Iver?" I asked. "Prut," said he unhesitatingly, but then he gave a start and looked at me with amazement in his eyes: "But this one is trailing a loose string!"

"Exactly," said I, "that's why I called for you, so that you could see it and draw your own conclusions."

With teeth chittering with cold we went back to the hut to discuss the strange thing: we had had two tame foxes in and around the hut, Fie and Prut, and now suddenly it looked as though there were three foxes, all of which had been in captivity. Where had the third one come from?

Out of our loneliness and longing for other people we concocted a wonderful explanation, namely that there must be people nearby who had caught the fox and had it on a string, and that it had got loose and come to us. Perhaps with a message? At all events we took it for granted that where a fox could come to us, the reverse must also be possible. So we made a fox's collar and fastened a cartridge to it and inside the cartridge put a message to the effect that we were living on Bass Rock and would very much like to get in contact with the other people, who must be somewhere near by. Then we caught a fox, put the collar on it and let it loose — as messenger to the people living on the coast, wherever they were, requesting a reply by fox messenger.

We waited in tense excitement, continually peering out of the door or window, while we kept saying how lovely it would be if, as we hoped, the morning brought news that a ship was lying frozen somewhere near us. That ship, of course, could be none other than *Laura* with her Austrian counts aboard: "And you'll see, Iver, where there are counts, there will be countesses as well!"

And so we waited in greater excitement than ever, waited for days for the answer that never came. That was strange, we felt, and, pondering the problem, we became silent and irritable, because we could not explain what we did not understand.

One day Iver began laughing in a way that I knew was the prelude to an unexpected, and usually unpleasant, question. It was a surprise too, when eventually he asked it: "Don't you think," he said, "that there's a danger our senses may be a bit queer? That we are seeing things that don't exist — and believing in something that isn't there?"

"Do you mean, that we're going off our heads?" I asked in amazement, and though he energetically denied having meant that, my question was not unjustified.

There may indeed have been something in it, for all our hopes exploded some days later when, determined to get to the bottom of the fox business for the sake of our peace of mind, we caught the foxes which we thought were messengers. It turned out that the foxes we caught, or shot, were our lodgers of the winter — and Prut was a fox we had not seen before.

That was a queer business, and we felt slightly ashamed when eventually we gave up hope of receiving a fox messenger from the ship with the counts and countesses. But, queer and shaming though it undoubtedly was, it was useful in that it gave us something to think and talk about at a time when life was pretty dismal.

And anyway it was of little importance whether we saw things or not. Winter raged itself out with a few violent storms that veiled everything in clouds of snow. Otherwise it was dead calm with ringing frost, sparkling stars and lovely northern lights flaring and billowing across the sky and giving a little light to the earth. And then there was also the moon to rejoice us; small and faint-hearted it was in its early phase, and scarcely noticed among the sparkling galaxy of the stars and waves of colourful Northern Lights. But it was the more welcome and dominant when it had grown to more than half, and glorious when at the full it sailed across the swarming throng of the stars, gleaming like freshly cleaned silver and enabling us to make longish trips into the mountains or across the sea, until it waned and was again swallowed up by the polar darkness that is more oppressive than storm or cold, more than loneliness and uncertainty.

We had been pleased to see the sun again after our first long winter night. We sent it a kindly nod as though it were an old friend whom we were welcoming home after a trip abroad. The next year, it was with ineffable joy and delight that we two freezing creatures had seen it return, shining blood-red through a veil of mist filled with ice crystals that gleamed and glittered in the air. Now, when for the third time we awaited its return, it was in a state bordering on worship. We stood, two shadowless figures, on the most southerly knoll, gazing out across the shadowless snowy landscape and waiting for the blaze in the south to be kindled and conjure blue shadows out of our dead world.

Iver and I were as silent as though at our devotions. We stood close together, our eyes on the horizon, where the blue of the sky and the white of the sea met. We stared across the dull white sea at the blue heavens and the conflagration away there in the south. The thin frost-smoke hanging over the open leads between the floes was fiery-red, and growing redder and redder. Then the blaze flared up violently; the colours became brighter and at the same time warmer, and then the veiling mist was split by a shaft of fire that dealt the long, dark polar night a mortal wound and stained the snow deep pink, as though with blood from some noble creature.

The sun had come back to us again!

We had no words to say. We just stood still and stared at the magnificence of it. The world had become so lovely, so alive with shadows and light, and even our sallow faces were brushed with a golden glow. Our breath was like fine mist in front of our mouths; it gathered around Iver's head — and, I suppose, round mine as well — like a halo, which glowed with all the colours of the rainbow.

Now that the sun was back we felt frisky and strong, and we determined to test our strength with a small sledge trip before we began preparing for a possible journey by boat and ice to Angmagssalik. As the weather seemed settled now that the sun was back, we put our shoulders into the traces and started off with high courage — and speedily regretted it, for unfortunately we discovered all too quickly that our strength was far from what it had been. The labour of pulling the heavy sledge was almost beyond us, and after two days it became more than we could manage, and we had to turn and go back.

As we could not pull the sledge even with a small load, there was no question of our being able to haul the load we should need to have if we were to try drifting south with the ice.

It was bitter to have to admit to ourselves that we were no longer able to do what, in our arrogance, we had thought would be relatively easy. Our hopes of being able to get away by ourselves were dashed completely, and we had to accept the fact that we must just wait for a ship to come and rescue us, wait a short time or a long, but just wait. And if the wait was a very long time, say another year, it would undoubtedly also be for all eternity.

We went to another small island, Walrus Island, and on the shore there we found a large piece of drift timber. Before leaving to return to Bass Rock we erected this piece of timber in a pile of stones, and I tried to carve our initials into the hard wood, so that any who might come that way would know where we were. My knife was not sharp enough to give the letters the depth necessary, if they were to be distinct and easily legible; nor did we have a pencil; but a rifle bullet being of lead proved serviceable, and, having rubbed one to a point on a stone, I was able to print on the white wood

E.M. BASS ROCK. 11/4. 1912

letters that perhaps were what saved us, for they were seen that summer by a sealer.

That done, we toiled back to our little, dark untidy hut and hoped that the summer of 1912 would be considerably better than the preceding one.

CHAPTER XIX

Hopes Fulfilled

*Bears and bear-hunting — I operate on my neck with a sheath knife —
Doubt and depression — What fools can quarrel over —
A ship comes — Journey and arrival home*

Over the years we had had a number of adventures with bears, honest, decent creatures on the whole, though often led into harm's way by their insatiable curiosity. I remember how once we sent a shot after a bear so far away that the bullet struck the snow a good way behind it. The bear, hearing the report of the rifle and the thud of the bullet, could not resist turning back to investigate. It walked towards us, snuffing as it came, as though bent on finding out what it was that had come flying after it.

That proved our opportunity and the bear's undoing, for we were able to come within proper range and also to get broadside on to it. Thus, the next time the rifle spoke, the bullet drove deep into the bear's chest.

Once — but that was the only occasion — it was touch and go with us. That was just after we had had to give up the plan of drifting south with the ice, and we had gone back to the hut on Shannon to leave word there that we were waiting for a ship on Bass Rock. A bear had taken up quarters in a snowdrift up against the hut, and when we arrived and began breaking up packing cases for firewood, the bear became angry and turned against us. Iver just caught a glimpse of the bear through the half-open door and hurriedly slammed it to. Unfortunately the door opened inwards, so Iver set his back against it to keep the brute out, shouting to tell me that a bear was attacking and that I must get ready to shoot as quickly as I could.

That, however, was easier said than done, for my rifle was frozen, the cartridges were frozen, and there was too much hoar-frost filling the chamber. When I loaded the rifle, the bolt would not close properly and I feared, certainly with every justification, that the locking mechanism would not hold if I fired a shot. So I seized an axe as my weapon against the bear, which was hissing and roaring wickedly, and playing such a tattoo on the door that we expected it to be sent flying into the hut at any moment. Iver was still braced against the door and yelling at me to get the rifle right.

Then there was a moment's quiet, and we breathed a sigh of relief and hoped that the bear had raised the siege; but that was a vain hope, for a few seconds later we heard it snarling just outside the hut and I realized that if it hit the door now, it would strike so hard that neither clasp, hinges nor Iver could keep the bear out.

It did strike hard, a decisive blow; yet before the door crashed in and Iver was flung across the hut, a pan of water spilled on to the red-hot coals in the stove, enveloping us in steam and smoke. I had already shouted to Iver to take his rifle and fire, but not to stop and look to see if it were loaded — and let's hope that it was! — and we were now standing side by side. Ten feet away was the bear with its forepaws inside the hut and a highly astonished look on its face, as it stared at a half-tumbled stove, a lot of sizzling embers and hissing steam, and two live creatures the like of which it had never seen.

Luckily Iver's rifle was loaded. In the confined space of the little hut the report was ear-splitting. When the bullet entered the bear's chest, the fur billowed like a field of corn under a gust of wind. The bear stood for a moment shaking its head dejectedly, then all at once it collapsed with blood gushing from the wound, its nose and its mouth, stone-dead. The tension had been considerable, and as the bear died we both subsided on to a packing case and sat there wiping off the sweat that had sprung out on our foreheads, even though cold air was pouring in through the open door from the sunlit outside and condensing into opaque mist in our dark and clammy den.

Spring came, and the migrating birds passed overhead on their way north to the plains of Shannon Island and the fertile land round Danmarks Havn. None settled on our Bass Rock, for there was only stone to be had there, none that is except the snow buntings which did not seem to mind its sterility. Those small pretty birds were a great joy and encouragement to us, as they hopped about, chirruping and pecking at the few blades of sprouting grass and picking up what oatmeal the hares had not had time to eat.

We both of us wanted livening up, for neither of us felt well. I had a nasty tumour on my neck, a sort of malignant boil that had plagued me since the darkest days of winter, and it was growing almost from day to day and hurting so badly that something had to be done. But what? Iver suggested hot compresses and we tried that, but the compresses became cold so quickly that they did not help, rather the reverse.

I had long been toying with the idea of cutting a hole in the tumour, for it was not a proper boil; but it is one thing to come to the conclusion that such a thing ought to be done, and quite another to put it into practice, especially with conditions as they were in our dirty hut. I knew, or thought I knew — which amounted to the same thing — that there was a network of nerves and sinews near the place where the tumour was largest. What would happen if I put a knife to my neck, pressed it in and perhaps severed those sinews and nerves? It seemed to me that the consequences might be disagreeable. Also I had no idea where the arteries were. Thus there was plenty to make one hesitate about such an undertaking.

Added to all these more or less real dangers, there was the further obstacle that I had nothing but my sheath knife with which to perform the operation. This was the knife I used at table, and it was also brought into service for skinning bear, or shaping a piece of wood or any other special purpose; but it was not especially sharp, and, though no doubt I could have found a stone that would have done as a whetstone, whenever I thumbed its rusty edge, as I did many times a day, I always decided to postpone matters.

Iver refused to have anything to do with the operation. If there was to be one, I must perform it myself. And always, just as I had made up my mind to do it, I found a fresh excuse to put it off: such as that we had no mirror, so that I could not see where I was making, or should make, the cut. When it comes to it, of course, you do not need such a thing; on a calm day a puddle can do instead — until the blood begins to flow; but that I only discovered, when it started dripping into the water.

I spent a day or two sharpening my knife and then, as the sun was shining and the air relatively warm, I had a dress rehearsal, mirroring myself in a puddle and drawing a piece of stick across the place on my neck where I considered the cut should be made. This was not easy; it is, in fact, quite difficult to follow direction in a reflected picture. Then, feeling I could wait no longer, I pulled myself together, gave the knife an extra whetting, nodded to Iver and saw that he had some cloth from an old tent ready for a bandage, stared at my image in the puddle and pressed the knife into my neck, finding to my amazement that I did not feel so very much. The moment the blood and pus began dripping into the puddle, the surface became ruffled and quite useless as a mirror. I had just sufficient presence of mind left to press the knife in and draw it downwards — then everything went dark, and Iver bandaged the wound as well as he could.

That operation brought me relief and the wound never became infected, but when I reached home a few months later and the doctors got hold of me, they shook their heads in horror and said something about only a fool being able to get away with what ten wise men would hesitate to do.

We were looking forward to the early summer; to the days when the ship could come, though for all our longing we had not been able to exorcize doubt with its insidious *if*. We tried to banish that horrible word from our minds — of course the ship would come — but it is easier to doubt than to believe, and by degrees, as high summer drew near and our expectations grew, we both became more nervy and irritable than we had ever been before. We realized that we could not endure another winter. Neither our health nor our minds could bear the heavy burden of another period of darkness, and also we had used almost all the provisions, clothes and ammunition which were absolutely essential for the maintenance of life.

We tried to keep ourselves busy with hunting, or we walked ourselves tired by continually going up the mountain to look at the ice, or rather the water between the ice. Conditions did not, in fact, look so bad, much better than the previous year, but a storm could dash all our hopes in the course of a few hours. And what then? The spectre of doubt was at once beside us whispering: "What will you do, *if* the ship cannot come in this year either? Will you take up the struggle for continued existence, or will you give up?"

We looked at each other and said nothing, for we each had difficulty enough in keeping our own thoughts in check. Silence under such conditions, however, was not good, for it could become oppressive and give birth to evil ideas. Nothing, of course, happened, or could happen, during those two months between spring and summer. We had to stay where we were, where we knew every stone, every light effect, every sound; thus an outside influence strong enough to break down any wall of silence that might arise between us was a most unlikely thing. Where could it come from? We had to be very wary, much more so than before, and although we had been alone together for nearly two and a half years without once quarrelling, it would not have taken much for us to have let slip some thoughtless word that would have been deeply wounding.

Our nerves were worn thin, thinner than ever before. We were hag-ridden by the fear of having to spend another year there, and each time we saw the scattered state of the pack ice and hope of the ship's arrival welled up within us, dreadful doubt was at once there whispering.

And then, of course, Iver must needs do what he should have avoided at all costs, and say things that shattered the calm for which we had struggled so hard. It was morning just as I woke. I was on the point of saying something comforting to Iver, who was standing at the stove making a sort of porridge that tasted awful but was filling; but I never got it said, for just at that moment Iver began singing a song I had not heard before, a song about my girl and me, that is the girl from the postcard, Miss Steadfast, my sweetheart.

I listened, surprised and rather hurt at my old friend's complete lack of loyalty; for the song that Iver must have composed during the night was an insult to my honour and that of my girl. There I sat in my sleeping bag, gazing in amazement at the singer stirring his porridge — and feeling a wall of silence growing up between us, an insurmountable wall behind which Iver stood, his stirring hand moving more and more slowly, while the smile in his eyes vanished and was replaced by an expression of sorrow and shame.

Iver passed me a bowl of porridge: "It's better today," he said with a little catch in his voice. I took the bowl without a word.

We ate our porridge without speaking, and not a word was said as we did the day's jobs. Then Iver went out, and I too went out and up on to the mountain and looked out across the ice; but never so much as a nod did I give the man who stood only a few yards away pretending to be looking across the ice as well, while he shot stealthy glances at me. We returned to the hut without having exchanged a word or even said that the ice looked better than the day before, a fact that normally would have made us jubilant.

Iver took exceptional pains with our bear-steak for dinner and handed it to me with a queer beseeching expression in his eyes. And I? Yes, I honestly did try to find the words that would break the barrier of silence, and I felt ashamed at being so silly, but I could not find anything to say, or to do, that would break the curse of silence.

When the time came, we crept into our sleeping bags without having said a word to each other all day long. I could hear that Iver lay awake most of the night, as I did too, filled with shame and despising myself for not having been able to find a word to break the horrible noose that silence had drawn round us and was pulling tighter and tighter.

When the sun was again peering in at our little window and it was time to turn out, we were still silent as we sat, each on his packing case, staring despondently into the air. In the end Iver stood up, wrote something on a piece of paper and went out.

All of a sudden I felt so utterly alone and forlorn that I shuddered. I was actually making for the door, intending at last to break the stupid, dangerous silence, when I heard Iver's feet crunching on the snow: he was coming back to the hut. Contrary to our habit he knocked on the door, hesitantly.

I knew what that meant and called: "Come in!" The first words either of us had spoken for almost two days. Then Iver opened the door ajar, threw a piece of paper in through the crack and said in a rather quavering voice:

"Here's a letter from Denmark!"

The next moment he was gone again and the door shut, but on the floor lay a piece of paper, shining and lifting the weight from my heart, for I knew what it meant and was: an apology for things said without thinking, a talisman that would extinguish the embers of smouldering hate and break the awful silence.

I picked up the little note and read: "I am so sorry I took your girl. Take her back, take my four as well, take the whole damned lot — only be cheerful again!"

And that was the man I had been on the point of hating! I suddenly wanted to see him, more than I have ever wanted to see anyone, and he was outside in the cold waiting anxiously for a word of friendship.

I spoke it and we laughed to each other, promising never again to let ourselves be caught in the evil circle of silence. Then Iver cooked a meal of the best the house could produce, which was not very grand. We sat on our packing cases looking happily at each other and thinking of our friendship that had held through the bad times when Death itself walked with us. To think that a few thoughtless silly words could have wrecked that friendship, had in fact done so for a few bitter hours, during which silence had grown up between us and our thoughts become malevolent.

Together we went up the mountain and looked out across the ice and the water, helping each other drive doubt underground, so that it left us in peace for some days. We again went hunting bear, hares or birds together, for our store of provisions had shrunk unpleasantly swiftly down to the bare minimum, and we had not had any fresh meat for some time. We were badly in need of fresh food, for our muscles were gradually stiffening, our joints growing tender, our gums red and swollen, our teeth loose. We were again threatened with scurvy.

We saw neither hares nor bear, not even a seal, but that did not make our need of meat any less; on the contrary, it grew and grew, until we wondered whether we ought not to have recourse to our last reserve, a flock of auks which had babies upon the mountain-side? We could not bring ourselves to that, however, so we tightened our belts instead, drank our coffee that smelt of carbolic and paraffin, smoked our stinking cigarettes, ate our musty biscuits and mildewed oatmeal, talked about the ship that could come any moment now, for the ice was broken and the sea navigable. The hour of our release must be at hand.

The next morning we decided that we would shoot the auks after all, and eventually we got them within range and in a place where the wind would make the dead bodies drift towards us. We lay side by side, looked at the auks and then peered out to sea in case there was a ship rounding the outer headland, which would have meant that the auks could have been allowed to live and go on giving their babies the food they were collecting for them with so much squawking.

How loud would not the squawking be, we thought, in a few hours' time, when the parent birds were in our pot? We could not bear the thought of the plaintive cries that would grow louder and louder and only stop, when the babies could cry no more and died of starvation. So we lowered our guns: "Let them live till tomorrow. We have gone hungry before. Perhaps a ship will come tonight."

We felt easy in our minds and proud of our magnanimous action as we walked back to our dark little hut, crept into our sleeping bags and said, as we had so many times before, perhaps the ship will come tonight?

Some hours later Iver was wakened by a commotion outside the hut. Thinking it was a bear rummaging among the cases and things we had lying outside, he seized his rifle — we badly needed meat now and a bear would be very nice to have. The commotion woke me as well and, seeing Iver making for the door with his rifle, I kicked my sleeping bag away, seized my rifle and ran barefoot for the door — which suddenly opened and outside we saw a group of men headed by a tall broad-shouldered chap who held out his hand: "Give us your rifles, boys, we come as friends."

Iver and I stood there side by side, each dressed in a thick woollen vest and nothing else but the rifles in our hands. We did not say a word, but put our rifles down and seated ourselves on the nearest case: the tension of two and a half years was over at last. Then words came, and the first were: "What a good thing we didn't shoot the auks yesterday!"

Then we said good-day to the big man and his companions. He was Paul Lillenaes, skipper and owner of *Sjøblomsten*, a little sealer which lay a short way out among the drifting ice on water that was alive with sun-glitter. He told us that he had been on his way home after an unsuccessful season on the coast of East Greenland, when he had sighted a piece of driftwood set up on the outer point of an island, and it had occurred to him that it might possibly have been erected by us to show that we were alive. He had lowered a dinghy and rowed ashore, seen the letters E.M. the date and Bass Rock, printed on the bleached wood — and known that in all probability he would return home with a profitable catch after all, for the Danish government had offered a reward of 10,000 Crowns to anyone who found us dead or alive, or who could supply satisfactory information as to our fate. That money was now his.

If *Sjøblomsten* had come eight days later, she would have been too late, for the Greenland Company's ship *Godthaab* was also on the East Greenland coast in 1912, landing I. P. Koch a little farther north, and on her return journey she touched at Bass Rock to see if she could find us, but we were then on our way to Norway.

According to our reckoning *Sjøblomsten* came on July 17, but apparently we had lost a couple of days somewhere on our travels. That was not really surprising, remembering that we had had to march day and night and just sleep when we could walk no farther. Two days were nothing compared with the 865 that Iver and I had spent alone together. Having discovered that our July 17 was the rest of the world's July 19, we skipped a couple of days in our diaries, called the day Thursday instead of Monday and were once more up to date.

It was a lovely day in the early morning of which *Sjøblomsten* arrived. The weather was as fine and summery, as befitted the happiness we all felt: Lillenaes and his crew at their "catch," and we at our rescue.

At first we could not realize that a ship really had come and that our lengthy solitude was over, and it only got properly into our heads when Lillenaes, smiling, said: "Well lads, put your clothes on and — let's go home!"

"Go home" — how sweet that sounded in our ears.

We had never thought of how we were dressed till then. They laughed and laughed as Iver struggled into his stiff sail-cloth trousers; and while they waited they had a look round our little hut. On one wall was a picture from a magazine: it was called "Four Generations" and depicted King Christian IX, Frederick VIII and Crown Prince Christian with his baby son in his arms, the present King Frederick IX.

"Well, he's dead now," said Paul Lillenaes, pointing to Frederick VIII. "And *Titanic* rammed an iceberg and went down with over a thousand lives lost. And the Danish East India Co. has built a large steamer that isn't a steamer at all, for it's supposed to be driven by a new kind of motor."

We were once more in touch with civilization, hearing news from the great world beyond East Greenland. And again we were objects of criticism, for a man came walking up from the shore and, when he saw our hut and our cooking utensils, he wrinkled his nose and said: "Ugh, what a mess!" We had never thought about the mess, but then the man was the little sealer's cook and steward. I had seen him first as the door opened, but only for an instant, for at the sight of us in our vests, rifle in hand, he had turned, run for the dinghy and jumped into it.

When he now returned to the hut I asked him in all innocence why he had run away the moment they found us. "And you ask that?" he said. "You would have run for it too, if you could have seen how dangerous you looked."

Maybe he was right; certainly Lillenaes and his men had thought we might be dangerous to approach, crazed by the solitude or something of the kind. "That was why I reached out for your rifles," Lillenaes told me later, "you can never tell what a lunatic with firearms will do."

While the Norwegians tidied the hut and the ground round it, Iver and I made a little tour of the place saying good-bye to our household gods — and feeling strangely restless and dull-witted. We could hardly realize that it was all over, that the time we had spent by ourselves, almost two and a half years, was now at an end. In all that long while we had stuck together; we had rejoiced together when there was anything to rejoice about; we had sighed together when the days and the outlook were black; we had starved together and frozen together; our lives had now and again hung on a thread, but only once had there been any real disagreement or enmity between us — and that over a girl on a postcard!

We now walked close together and nodded for the last time to all the stones we knew so well, to the mountains, to Shannon in the distance, where we had suffered such grievous disappointment the year before, and to the ever-changing pack ice. But all the while we kept one eye on the little sealer and laughed joyfully: so the ship had come after all — now our journey home could begin in earnest.

From the mountain-side we heard the peeping of the baby auks and angry screeches, and the parent birds were continually flinging themselves off the nests and diving for more food, the air whistling in their wings as they passed. Iver and I looked at each other, and I believe we were both thinking the same thing: Perhaps the ship came last night because we spared the birds yesterday.

So perhaps Paul Lillenaes was right in thinking that the loneliness might have made us a bit peculiar.

As we rowed out to the ship, I looked back at my dear Greenland, while Iver feasted his eyes on little *Sjøblomsten*. Suddenly he nudged me. His eyes were round with amazement: "Look there!" he said. "There are more of them yet!" He pointed at the ship, where five men stood to receive their strange passengers: first, seven men ashore, then five on board, that made twelve in all! Iver was right, it was a whole host that had invaded Bass Rock.

The engine room telegraph rang and the ship woke to life and began moving ahead. A few days later we saw the mountains of Norway above the eastern horizon, then wooded islets with pretty, little cottages, rowboats filled with waving smiling people, a town, Aalesund, and to port a fisherman's house with a girl in a red dress standing in the doorway, shading her eyes with her hands to get a better view of the weird strangers who were arriving. And Iver seized my arm in a fierce grip and said: "Look, there's a real girl!"

She was real all right, and when we got ashore there were others, many more. There was quite a crowd of them on the quay, all come to see if there were truth in the rumour that somehow or other had arrived ahead of *Sjøblomsten* — for those were the days before wireless — the rumour that she was coming home with a good catch: two men who for two and a half years had lived as Robinson Crusoe and Man Friday on the harsh coast of East Greenland.

It was an extraordinary experience having a bath again after three years, and the town's hairdresser had a remarkable experience when he had to remove our wigs of matted reindeer hair, grease and other things, a difficult task which was closely watched through the window by a collection of joyous children.

Telegrams arrived — one of the first was from King Christian IX — telegrams from family and friends, from many people whom we knew and did not know, an overwhelming number. We had new outfits to replace the weird garments we had made for ourselves out of sail-cloth and bits and pieces of cloth and skins. The sun shone, birds twittered, the trees were green and lovely flowers grew in the garden where the Danish consul welcomed us back to life with a glass of champagne.

Two days later we reached Copenhagen with the Oslo boat: a skipper without a ship and an engineer without an engine. Our companions, whom we had last seen on the inland ice, were there to welcome us, as were the members of the Committee in top hats, a couple of ministers, one of the King's secretaries, and two sets of parents standing staring up at the bridge and the two sons they had long since given up for lost, but who were now miraculously restored to them.

Given up? I wonder.

I was told later that father had gone to meet every Greenland boat that came to Copenhagen and had asked for news from Greenland — of the two who had not come back. But there never was any news, and father had walked away from the ship and the little crowd of happy parents come to welcome sons home from Greenland, his head well up. And mother? I do not know whether she had given me up, but I scarcely think so. She did not like to speak of the long time when she had not heard from me and must have suffered. The treasurer of the Committee, however, told me that when he received the telegram announcing our arrival at Aalesund, he naturally telephoned at once to my parents' home; Mother answered and he gave her the happy news.

"But she never asked for details," said the treasurer, "and I was rather surprised when, after a short silence, she interrupted my well-meant congratulations to ask: 'Are they both there?' I thought that a strange question coming from your mother, to whom the fact that you had come home must surely have been the main thing."

Perhaps. Later, I told mother what the treasurer had said and she explained why she had asked that question. "Naturally I was happy that you had come back — that was my immediate thought. And very happy. But then I thought of Iversen's mother — and that I should have rather you had not come back — than that you should have come back without him!"

Poor Mother, she had a hard time of it during those two years when our fate was undecided, for she had gradually come to know enough about conditions on journeys of that kind to be able to imagine it all. And that, too, was why she was not able to rejoice at my homecoming until she knew that we were both safe.

I said nothing, for I understood Mother; only my thoughts went back to an incredibly distant past when hunger, pain and exhaustion had almost overpowered us — and Iver had asked me to carry our one and only rifle.

Postscript

Time and again I have been asked what North-east Greenland is like, and now I have tried to answer that question. As I have described it in this book, such was North-east Greenland when it was discovered, explored and mapped, and such it must have been for millions of years since it was first clothed in its cap of ice and life there was exterminated. I in my simplicity never doubted that it would remain thus for all eternity: a harsh and desolate land without any means of supporting life, for even the Eskimos on the coast had died out.

That I was so utterly wrong in my view of North-east Greenland's eternal immutability was due first and foremost to the invention and improvement of the internal combustion engine. At the beginning of this century the petrol engine was a heavy, clumsy and unreliable thrall in man's service, yet in the course of a couple of decades it became the master of mankind or, at least, a fantastic creator of the energy without which the modern society cannot exist.

Directly or indirectly the motor plays a part in all man's undertakings. It makes electricity and provides the power that drives huge ships across the seven seas, and, amongst many other things, it has been the cause of clever technicians being able to realize man's oldest and most fantastic dream and hankering: to rise into the air and conquer space.

From the time the principle of the first aeroplane was discovered its development has been explosive, until we have arrived at the machines of today that fly at a thousand miles an hour and more and are driven by engines of tens of thousands of horse power.

The modern aeroplane upset a not very gifted prophet's view of the immutability of the status of North-east Greenland and reduced his eternity to a few decades, or to be exact from 1910, when I still believed that there were things that could endure for ever, until about 1950 when one such lone monster went flying over the desolate country round the mouth of Danmarks Fjord, where I had experienced the most bitter hours of my long life and seen the expected number of my days shrink to a few weeks, months at the most.

In the belly of this monster were comfortable, soft chairs in which sat officials, who, as they flew along at a low but safe height, looked for level stretches of ground in the wilderness. Those men had the power and the intention to violate the immutability of the wilderness and say where they could and should build a landing-ground, thus putting an end to the abiding desolation.

They found what they sought near the place where Iver and I had rested in 1910 and spoken frankly of the future, that for us could scarcely be a future at all. Once the site of the landing-ground had been fixed, a host of other huge aeroplanes followed in the wake of the first, winging their way from Thule across the inland ice to that place on the most northerly and most desolate coast of East Greenland, which those officials had selected. These new 'planes brought technicians and craftsmen who marked out the site of a whole little town, and this was built with materials brought from Thule by air, two thousand tons or thereabouts.

By the following year there had been built in the wilderness a town with a landing ground for large aeroplanes, a power station and wireless station with its cobweb of shiny copper wires stretched between tall wireless masts, from which messages could reach every country in the world with the speed of thought.

Scattered about the ground were warm, well-built houses with central heating and all that goes with a modern society, including a telephone from house to house, a hobbies workshop and a billiard saloon.

When all was ready and the houses furnished, thirty young Danes were flown to that, the most northerly weather and telegraph station in the world, and there they soon settled down and attended to their jobs just like their less adventurous fellow-countrymen at home in Denmark.

Once a month a 'plane from Thule touches down on the landing ground at Station North, so that its staff can get their letters, newspapers and small trifles that may have been forgotten, and at Christmas a 'plane, like a modern Father Christmas, brings presents to all the young men in what once was desolate land.

Each summer an aerial bridge seven hundred miles long is thrown across the inland ice from Thule to Station North, in order to supply those dwellings in the wilds, for there is no other way in which the 600 tons of food and other things required may be conveyed there. As well as these supplies, oil for the motors and central heating must be taken there, and materials for repairing this and that, or replacements for those who may have had enough of life in the wilderness and wish to exchange it for the noise and attractions of the city.

Not even the winter-darkness is what it used to be, for light from electric lamps pours from innumerable windows, and electric lights are hung between the houses, so that those who are abroad run no risk of losing their way in the dark.

It is only forty-odd years since Iver and I lay in a tent very near that spot, speaking gravely of life and death and presuming that the desolation we saw all round us would remain complete and utter as it was for all eternity. The fantastic development that has taken place was as impossible to foresee in 1910 as it would be to count the myriads of the stars twice and get the same result.

The improbable is nonetheless a reality now — and the impossible has been made possible by the magic powers of technique, especially of the motor.

Danmarks Havn lies some seven hundred miles to the south of Station North, and when we two famished and exhausted wayfarers in 1910 stumbled across the level grassy expanse towards the tumbledown little hut that to us represented the height of all earthly magnificence and security, it seemed to us that we had reached an oasis in the wilds.

We found the countryside lovely and good, but never in our wildest imagination could we have dreamed that about 1950 there would be built at that very place a large meteorological station, the staff of which looked in amazement at the remains of our little hut and indulgently shook their heads as much as to say: Fancy people being able to live under such conditions!

Iver and I were very glad of those conditions, but we can also well understand the wondering shakes of the head of those young people, for they have a chef employed at Station North to cook their food and bake their bread, and they are waited upon by an immaculate mess boy. They live in large warm houses that have no leaks or draughts; they have motors and electricity to work for them on the big wireless station from which — as from ten other Greenland meteorological stations — detailed weather reports are daily sent to Copenhagen, which then passes on to the meteorologists of Northern Europe the basic information on which to work out the weather forecast for the following day, forecasts which play an important part for almost all our activities, not least for the pilots of the big transatlantic air runs, who study the weather charts so as to get an idea of the weather they are likely to encounter on the long flight between the two hemispheres.

Desolate East Greenland has thus acquired great importance for civilized Northern Europe, and the clever author of the age-old "Mirror of the King" song has been proved right in his assertion that the weather that Northern Europe has, comes from Greenland whose "ice-crowned pate" makes the winds and weather in Iceland and Europe. The internal combustion engine had to be invented before we could see that the ancient bard was right about Greenland's influence on the weather, and act accordingly.

To the parts where Iver and I waited so long for a ship, each year now brings several motor vessels with relief crews and supplies for the Danish weather-reporting stations along the coast. Other ships come with the scientists who for the last thirty years have been working in the lovely fjords of East Greenland, investigating the land's flora and fauna and, not least, its geological structure.

Other Danish and Norwegian vessels come with more or less experienced trappers who, with the blessing and support of the Government, try to wrest from the skinflint land enough for a livelihood — but for all their industry there is little butter for their daily bread. Among these experienced, purposeful men you will also find young adventurers, who have taken jobs for a year or two to be trappers and hunt bears and foxes, shoot musk oxen and birds.

The northern coast of East Greenland is thus almost crowded nowadays, and although the trappers could never have kept going without economic support from the Danish and Norwegian governments, they have now built a large number of huts all along the coast from Danmarks Havn to Scoresby Sound — either quite large huts in which several men can live under more or less comfortable conditions, or small huts lying close enough together for the trapper to be able to journey from one to the other without much equipment, when he wants to inspect his fox traps.

The small huts are only intended for one person, and some of them only provide a rather miserable shelter; but nonetheless there are now huts all along the coast, and for those accustomed to that sort of travel and who do not expect too much in the way of comfort, there can nowadays be little difficulty in journeying by ski or sledge from Danmarks Havn to Scoresby Sound.

The plan that Iver and I hugged and brooded over in our solitude and aching longing for other people, was actually put into effect in 1924–25, when the country's own children, Greenlanders from Angmagssalik, were given the opportunity to live at the newly created colony at Scoresby Sound, from which, either alone or as sledge-guides for Danish scientists, they have made long journeys northwards along the coasts on which their ancestors travelled, hunted and lived in the olden days long before Europeans came.

On the mighty fjord that is Scoresby Sound there now live some 350 Greenlanders who all came from round Angmagssalik, and good wooden houses have been built here and there along the coast, often on the ruins of old dwellings. These houses are generally grouped in small communities, where the women and children live their placid lives in continual waiting for the breadwinner to return with the catch that his luck, cunning or strong arm has got either on land or ice or in the sea.

Thus the dream of the two solitary men, that it might be possible to see happy Eskimos by that southern headland, is now a reality. The men are there, and their wives and children too. Only the women's boat has disappeared as a result of changed conditions. Nowadays, the laughing Eskimo women pull at the oars of a clumsy boat of European origin, a craft far less well suited to East Greenland conditions than the cleverly constructed women's boat, the Eskimos' own ingenious invention that was used by them for centuries. Or an outboard motor may drive the boat across the sea with water foaming at the bows. The buzz of the motor is our mechanized age's modem accompaniment to the age-old travelling songs of the Eskimo.

A little to the north of Scoresby Sound is Kong Oscars Fjord, whose waters are so calm and sunny in the summer; it is a place of wild mountains, yet there is more noise of powerful motors there, than anywhere else along those coasts that once were so quiet. Winter and summer Danish engineers are using motor-made power and high explosives to drill and blast their way into the mountains, where their greedy arms scoop out the mineral deposits, which Danish geologists have found and which have been lying hidden deep within the East Greenland mountains ever since the flaming inferno of the world's beginning.

The din of big stone-crushers throbs out far across the land, and strings of lorries drive down to the shore where powerful motor-vessels lie waiting to take the wealth of East Greenland through the pack ice and across the Atlantic to the refineries of Europe.

Even the busy spoilt people from the big cities of Europe and America are beginning to acquire a slight personal knowledge of the wild coastal mountains of East Greenland and of the glistening inland ice, now that giant 'planes carrying scores of passengers wing their way across Greenland as they fly from one continent to the other.

As the 'plane roars along above those desolate stretches the pampered passengers sit in their soft armchairs, eating delicious food or drinking cocktails, perhaps dozing, or being bored and looking out of the window in search of distraction, they shake their heads despairingly: "Good God, what a country!"

It may happen that someone with an inquiring mind looks down at the inland ice or at the mighty coastal mountains, and even gives a thought to those who half a century ago did the pioneer work in the land below him, struggling forward foot by foot across the inland ice or following the tall riven coastal mountains in a boat or by sledge — people who were silly enough to think that the land that even from 15,000 feet looks so grim and awful, would remain desolate and uninhabited "for all eternity."

So many unexpected things have happened in East Greenland during the last fifty years, and especially in the last thirty, that the few men who knew the country in its original state and thought that it would stay like that for ever, have had to admit that nowadays everything is possible.

The pioneers would have needed the imagination of a romancer to have been able to foresee that within a few years that poor, harsh and desolate land would become a bone of contention between two brother nations, and that before forty years had passed, a Danish military unit would be stationed on its coasts.

That, however, was what happened: the former when Norwegian trappers in an act of youthful presumption occupied parts of East Greenland and aroused a wave of popular feeling in Norway which then claimed sovereignty over the country that all other nations regarded as a Danish colony, and which had been mapped and explored very largely by Danes, those who could not stay quietly at their own safe firesides.

The matter was settled by the International Court in the Hague which pronounced the stretches of coast in dispute, in fact the whole coast of East Greenland (as, indeed, the whole of Greenland) to have been Danish always, so that it must remain under Danish sovereignty, until — no, perhaps not until the end of time, that is a thing you can no longer assert in our breathless age, when developments that before took thousands of years are now accomplished in so very few.

When the second world war had been raging a year or two, we in Denmark heard vague incredible rumours of a small Danish army in East Greenland, of warlike preparations and even actual fighting there.

I had been able to understand and accept previous events on those coasts, even the squabbling between Denmark and Norway over the inheritance of their remote ancestors' right to Greenland, but these reports of warfare on the coast of North-east Greenland seemed quite unnatural and impossible, and I felt that they must be lies and invented, misunderstandings of rumours brewed in the cauldron of the war atmosphere.

But when Fate intervened and took me to America in the autumn of 1944 and shortly afterwards landed me in Greenland, to my immeasurable surprise I saw with my own eyes that the reports were true. What I had thought quite inconceivable was nonetheless a fact, even though the Danish Greenland "force" consisted only of eight men, of whom four were officers, three N.C.O.s and only one a private.

This little force, surely the smallest in the world, for all its size and extraordinary composition, had done good service in skirmishes with the Germans who had established a meteorological station on Sabine Island, which sent back weather reports to Germany so that the pilots of Hitler's bombers could have some idea in advance of what the weather would be like when they went to bomb the towns and cities of England.

There was a "battle" in which the Danes were defeated. One N.C.O. was shot and the Germans burned the Danish HQ and presumably thought that thereby they had made themselves masters of East Greenland. There, however, they were wrong, for the Danes were good sledgers and knew the country; they made their way to Scoresby Sound as fast as they could, and from there wirelessed to the Americans on Iceland giving them the position of the German weather-reporting station on Sabine Island.

The Americans did not need telling twice, but acted straightaway. A squadron of bombers took off at once and shortly afterwards fire and bombs were raining down on the German buildings which went up in flames, and a German ship that lay frozen-in in the harbour was sent to the bottom. That was the end of that meteorological station, for its crew disappeared mysteriously, presumably on board a 'plane they had summoned. Weather reports from East Greenland were of such importance to the Germans, however, that they again tried to set up a station, this time on Shannon Island, at *Alabama*'s old winter harbour. They were not left in peace there either. The Danes found them, and although there were about thirty Germans, the six Danes made a night attack. They shot a German officer who surprised them, but had to withdraw when they were subjected to murderous fire. They got away, however, thanks to their familiarity with the country and its conditions.

The wireless did the rest, and as soon as a ship could slip through the pack ice, the Americans were there with men and a gun, but they arrived too late: the Germans had again been evacuated by 'plane, and the only traces of them the Americans found were an empty house and the wreck of their boat which lay crushed in the ice, frozen fast to the land.

That was a great disappointment for the Americans, but Fate made up for it when one of their reconnaissance 'planes located a fresh German landing on Little Koldewey, the same island that had stood like a black silhouette in the middle of the midday glow, when Iver and I, forty years before, had sat in the little hut at Danmarks Havn gazing longingly through the window in the vain hope of seeing the others coming.

That meteorological station had to be wiped out at any price, and in the middle of October with its cold, storms and darkness, a large new American icebreaker with engines that developed 12,000 h.p. forced her way through the pack ice and reached the island, where the Americans completely surprised the Germans and took them all prisoner, and sank a German expedition ship with gunfire. The icebreaker herself, however, made a good target for an enemy U-boat that happened to be there and it fired two torpedoes, which luckily both exploded in the ice. The U-boat then disappeared.

Shortly afterwards the icebreaker's own 'plane spotted yet another German expedition ship lying frozen in severe pack ice, where she seemed to be safe from enemy attack. The captain of the icebreaker thought otherwise, and he did in fact get his ship through the ice and reached the other, which had to surrender. The most northerly naval battle in history thus ended in a decisive victory for the Americans — it was, indeed, a considerable feat.

When I came to Greenland I met this icebreaker's commander, Commander Charles W. Thomas, at the American base at Julianehaab, and it was he who told me about the military actions on the East Greenland coast and of the sea-fight by night off Koldewey Island, a thrilling story.

But as he was telling it to me, he suddenly broke off and said: "But I had almost forgotten that you know these parts. I have read your book, and I imagine that to you, one of the pioneers in the country, what has happened must seem a very strange, and probably also a very regrettable, development: that a desert and newly-discovered country should be turned into a theatre of modern warfare with aeroplanes, wireless and great activity."

The Commander was right: inconceivably much has happened in East Greenland since Iver and I fought our way along its coast in 1910. The land that I considered must, for good or evil, remain untouched by civilization till the world's end, has in the course of a few years become one of civilization's stamping grounds: the motor has triumphed over the wilderness and its hum can be felt, almost heard — throughout those wide lands, where before silence was a thing that was almost palpable.

The motor has had its day and good use has been made of it. Now, I suppose, we have the age of the atom and new fantastic forces are being developed. In ten years time motors will be antiquated, thrust aside by other inventions that will be stronger and have an even greater effect on all aspects of life.

Anything can happen now, everything is possible and one no longer dares to say of even the most fantastic statement about new technical inventions: that is impossible! I have long given up my view that East Greenland must remain the desolate and empty land that Iver and I knew, and which we liked, despite the bitterly hard conditions it offered two wayfarers.